SAVE

ONE

CHILD

IAN JAMES

A Wild Wolf Publication

Published by Wild Wolf Publishing in 2018
Copyright © 2018 Ian James

ISBN: 978-1-907954-68-9
Also available as an ebook

www.wildwolfpublishing.com

PROLOGUE

Spring 2006

'You had better come home and look at this,' my wife Julie rang me at work to say.

'There's a letter here for you.'

I had completely forgotten that someone had contacted me two years previously to tell me I had been recommended but by now I had realistically put it out of my mind.

Many had been here before me and plenty would follow in the future. To be put forward was more than enough. I was well aware that not everybody made it past nomination.

I knew that New Year of 2005 would have been too soon but equally there had been the two half-yearly occasions since when people were recognised. The moment had passed, I felt.

Besides, I had only been doing my job after all.

But when Julie called, for some reason I made a lame excuse at the station that I had to take the eight-mile journey home and see what was so important. My wife understood the importance of my work better than anyone and indeed had endured long periods when she simply couldn't get hold of me at all, so recognising the smile in her voice and that there was nothing urgent – but there also was – I made my excuses and disappeared from the office.

When I arrived home, she was convinced that I had already guessed. The truth was that I was clueless. In fact, I read the letter three times.

I was speechless.

I had no idea what to think or what to do except that I had to respond to it.

And when I returned to work...

'Everything okay at home?' a colleague asked.

'Everything just fine,' I replied as I had done so many times over the years when I walked back in as though nothing had happened from my time away on operations.

The truth was that *lots* had gone on. Much of it was unspoken outside of the covert arena of policing, because being a policeman's lot was simply a life of things you needed to know and those you didn't. The nature of my job was that work was always fishing a little as to where I had been or what I had done, and I would rarely give them a sniff. That was in their professional mentality and it had become part of my other identity. I knew not to give an inch.

This time though, I was grinning. Yet, still disinclined to expand. I had become for real the confidential discreet character I had learned to play. That afternoon I simply resorted to type and carried on with my workload as I had done so frequently in the past, regardless of the circumstances I had emerged from.

When I had a moment to reflect, it became obvious that my name would appear in the press and everyone would start to ask questions – from my own children to my neighbour to those people whose noses I had been working under for years without their knowledge.

I became anxious wanting to know what was going to be released to the media, which would or may have a bearing on highlighting what I did.

I called the relevant office in London who had sent me the letter:

'Because of my role, I am worried what will be said on the day.'

'Don't worry,' came the response. 'Your name will be released to the press agencies, but the award will be listed simply as services to the police.'

My apprehension began to subside.

I was also told there would be no photo of me available.

I then contacted a senior officer at New Scotland Yard who was responsible for Covert Policing and confided that I was going to accept. This was not a unique situation, though of course it felt so to me. He had shielded officers before me in similar circumstance. I was again given assurances that the reality of what I done would not be released to the public and he offered his congratulations and stated it was much deserved.

I couldn't allow myself to get carried away with what the day itself might entail. It was still some way off. It took me a further fortnight to reply in writing, let alone going to see my own senior officer. I waited a further couple of weeks just sitting on it, letting the dust settle.

And that was Mark, Detective Chief Superintendent Head of Crime whom I had worked with and known for a lot of years. I didn't need to worry. Unlike others he was the soul of discretion.

'That's absolutely fantastic,' he beamed when I showed him the letter.

'It's not official yet but will be released in a few weeks.' I told him and with that, I kept my counsel small.

I knew my Dad would have been a very proud man. It was his wise words of wisdom that encouraged me to leave Cornwall in search of a trade that took me here.

And here meant Buckingham Palace.

On a daily basis, I was a professional doing what I trained for and what was asked of me in the moment. In the cold light of day, I was elated that Her Majesty the Queen had chosen to award me an M.B.E.

It meant that it had all been worth it. Not for me, but for all those who had the vision to see that my role was necessary and for all those who were consequently saved as a result.

My work had been tough, gruelling, stressful and riddled with risk against some of the most manipulative people in society and it was my job to stop them whilst living with the emotional scars but marking fine lines between my professional and my home life.

My work was unique and specialist. Only a handful of us did this type of service.

Now my family and I were going to see the Queen.

My life undercover was about to emerge at the surface.

I had been a paedophile.

But only in the name of duty.

And when Dad said all those years ago to head to London and that there was nothing for me in Penzance, neither of us could have imagined what that truly meant.

1

I was born in Penzance in 1959. You almost cannot get further off the coast of England. That also meant you were pretty detached from opportunity. My father worked in milk distribution for a creamery; Mum worked in a primary school and the catering business.

Fishing, tin mining or tourism. They were the options. Though, somehow my younger sister went on to set up her own online pet business.

I had always fancied being a fireman after I watched in horror in 1967 as the Torrey Canyon oil spill wrecked many of these life choices in one fell swoop. Close to 36 million gallons of crude oil devastated the Cornish coast and beyond it lay what remains the UK's worst such disaster in history. Many people I knew suffered and lost their livelihood.

Amidst this DNA emerges my story.

There was one other alternative, of course.

'There's nothing for you here,' Dad had said. 'You need to get a secure job.'

So I activated Plan B. And left.

By the age of seventeen, I had abandoned school with a few CSEs and a love of sport. Through my passion for table tennis, I had glimpsed another world simply by travelling and competing around England and Wales.

But that was it. I knew little else of the outside world – the real world. In Cornwall just making your way across a pedestrian crossing, everything stopped.

I was apprehensive but excited about leaving.

'They are recruiting everywhere,' Dad had said. 'People from all over the place are joining.'

I hadn't thought too much of it except that I agreed that it was a career and that opportunities were limited if I stayed. There is no way that what was about to unfold would have happened if I had chosen to stay.

Within no time I found myself positively miles away – in Exeter! After initial exams there, came the home visit. They had to verify who I was and run quick tests on my eyesight and perform a general medical, but that was essentially it. In 1977, none of the checks of today nor the requirement to tick equality boxes existed. It was open season for hiring and I sailed through, and before I knew it, just my suitcase and I were making the six-hour train journey to London for a new life from which there would be no return. Apart from visits and family occasions, I never really went back.

Dad was right.

I undertook an initial six-month cadet process and then like many before I went to Hendon. The new surroundings – London – and the size of the Metropolitan Police did not faze me but there was that silent pressure sitting on my shoulder that I could not muck this up. I couldn't return a failure and there *was* nothing to go back for. My *journey* was, in every sense, a one-way ticket.

I sensed an adventure too. Anything could happen. One thing was clear, though. For the first time in my life, I was now part of a professional body and had to play by their rules. I had not been a wild child in any sense and much of my sporting success was in individual pursuits rather than in a team so this was literally a whole new ball game.

I was to become a policeman.

That meant you had to take a bit of your own brain out and be moulded. They were strict on sexual orientation and were keen on the tone you adopted. It was a different type of discipline all together and it was their way. Knowing the difference between right and wrong was key.

My first day was in April 1978 and the Met began the process of imposing *them* on me. Corporate identity struck its first blow at the barbers. I had neither short nor long hair but a crew cut conditioned me to type. We marched everywhere too.

I was keen to be me. I wanted my own identity without getting lost in the system whilst realising there *was* a lot on offer here. I suspect that the path my career ultimately took exemplifies just that. I learned to respect the traditions, culture and standards of the police but I somehow wanted to carve my own niche within it.

It was the kind of job where you could be despised or held in high regard in equal measures but from my own character and from my initial mentees, I believed in honesty, integrity and treating people fairly. Without it having been my lifelong ambition to become a cop, I felt instantly that it was right and suited my personality.

I had ten weeks of training at Hendon. Most of it was about the law. Around me were many similar starters aged between 18 and 23. I remember two things stood out. The legislation per se was much bigger than I thought and it hit home how the Police was generally seen as the enemy.

And my first assignment exposed everything about having come from Cornwall. I was posted to Stoke Newington – a multi-cultural part of London, home to 90% black community with the rest made up of Irish, Asian, Jewish and European descent. The famous Kray Twins had once owned this patch. I was thrown straight into the deep end. Outside of Brixton, Stoke Newington and the surrounding areas of Hackney, Dalston, Finsbury Park and Tottenham were regarded at the time as the toughest areas to police.

Despite that demographic, your officer on the beat remained mostly white. Black officers were largely considered 'Judas' by their own communities. I had barely seen anybody dark-skinned in Penzance let alone violence on such a graphic scale. The idea of being glassed in a West End nightclub and returning home with 40 stitches as I had during training was a world away.

This was the real thing – and around the corner in 1981 such tensions spilled over three years later into the notorious Brixton Riots. This coincided with large full on disturbances in Stoke Newington and the nearby districts.

But I loved Stoke Newington and my new life. I settled in well and made several friends who remain loyal to this day, despite the passage of time and life's course sending us in different directions. That was true friendship and camaraderie. Plenty of laughs and good times.

Being single and living in a Section House that overlooked the rear of the Police Yard, you were never far from the sirens, the smell of manure from the horses and of course those prisoners shouting and causing havoc. You quickly became immune to it and it became your life.

There was an early marker too. I was mentored well by a guy who took time to look after me and about whom I could not say a bad word. Years later, he himself undertook an armed robbery in Kent with a sawn-off shotgun. Sometimes the two worlds of cop and crook would come to merge.

I did not see it as a badge of honour at the time because I was just doing my job and proud of it, but I suppose every officer is asked if they can remember their first arrest. Mine was on my first day and a prostitute in Finsbury Park. They were everywhere and it was not a difficult moment. But I had started and was getting into the role. Reading somebody their rights comes naturally over time. On day one, you have to check yourself.

And so, it had begun. The uniform policeman making arrests for crime, learning from my colleagues and engaging with the public and every now and again it was off to police the football. Sometimes it was Arsenal one weekend and Tottenham the next, followed by supporting officers at West Ham and of course not to mention demonstrations in Central London. This made up much of my probationary period of 18 months before a six-month secondment to a beat unit which dealt with low level crime of mostly assaults, criminal damage and theft.

It was at Stoke Newington that I experienced that moment every London cop will do at some point – increasingly nowadays. I had never seen anybody die on me in my life.

One evening I took a call to attend a kebab shop in the High Street. They needed my First Aid skills from my cadetship. There was nobody else to hand. I arrived to find a customer screaming in Greek – his leg all but hacked off with a slicing knife from the takeaway. Pain is the same in any language.

I had covered his leg with tea towels, stopping the bleeding, and while he went to the hospital with the paramedics I was then sent home, myself covered in his blood. Obviously I knew I had done a good job because he lived. More significantly for me, this was new territory and I *was* excited, or perhaps exhilarated is better. It was instinct. You just went in and did it. No time to think what if.

Every police officer experiences that buzz and it is a quirk of humanity that it mostly evolves in our work through negative circumstance but this was *my* first such moment and I wanted more *in*volvement.

It was proof that Stoke Newington and the job were not for the faint-hearted. You had to learn hard and you had to learn fast. From day one, we were always encouraged to engage with the public of whatever age, whether in the street, shops, cafes and community centres. Some would blank you and others would chat. In time some would realise that you and the force were actually decent.

Stokie, as it was affectionately known, was an area full of crime. Murders were plenty. Robberies incurred violence. Drugs were all over the place. Stabbings were almost normal given that everyone seemed to carry a knife and were not afraid to use one. It did really hit home how dangerous it was. Flick and Stanley knives would carve your face open let alone slice a handbag or steal a purse.

Yet, I found myself being drawn towards this crime and investigating it. Important but mundane work like traffic was something I kept at arm's length and did not interest me, much to the amusement of my supervisors.

By 1979, I had my first real taste of court. Carrying out police work was one massive job. Recounting it in front of a judge some months or years later was obviously vital to the process. There was no point in patrolling the streets and reading people their rights if your demeanour betrayed that process – and I fell woefully short at my initial appearance. I never forgot this lesson, especially with what lay ahead.

Required to deal with an adjournment at Horseferry Magistrates Court in connection with an Actual Bodily Harm charge before a Stipendiary Magistrate, I went alone. So alien was the process, I really should have not done so or at least made myself more aware. It was not the words that I spoke but my understanding of the whole theatre of it which let me down, and afterwards I was duly bollocked. I had given evidence, but this was different. I was the officer in charge of the case.

'Don't ever come to court again, if you don't know what you are doing,' said the Detective Sergeant afterwards.

He had earlier been forced to step into the witness box and uttered the words 'request an adjournment for case papers to be prepared for trial' to cover for me. I was that bad.

I never wanted to be in that situation again. Next time, I wanted to thrive but the truth was I had been left squirming.

I resolved to get better. One crime resonated with me. A little girl aged six years old was playing in the street when a sixteen-year-old boy threw a brick and it caught her full on in her eye. Normally this would have gone to the Criminal Investigation Department (C.I.D) because it was a wounding. However, it was initially processed to me and I saw the case through to its conclusion, arresting the youth concerned, attending Moorfield Eye Hospital and gathering the evidence. Only after several operations did the girl recover and regain her sight.

This one incident had got me noticed and impressed detectives, who this time oversaw the matter with me at court. Looking back, I feel they made a mental note.

As a consequence, I was given my first 'move' within Stoke Newington. I had one foot in the world of being a detective and so I joined the Robbery Squad and subsequently the Crime Squad.

My experiences were soon both comic and tragic:

I began by following a lad in Sainsbury's who had been seen snatching a handbag and dived on him to such a degree that he found himself at the exit with his trousers at his ankles. He was doing anything he could to escape and we had already caused carnage in the aisle so to subdue him I managed to grab a tin of peas and wacked him, giving me enough time to cuff him. The youth was so strong and over six feet tall but turned out to be only sixteen.

Naturally, I became the subject of a few jokes to my embarrassment, but it was very much the case that if you couldn't take a joke then you shouldn't have signed up. That was the mentality.

I loved my time on the Robbery Squad running observations, following suspects intent on doing snatches on buses, or at bus stops and busy streets. Of course, we had our own language too like 'Dipping' now known as pickpocketing. Suspects therefore were Dippers! At times the cases were complex because not only was everyone in Stoke Newington at it but active criminals outside the area would come in and operate! Therefore, a lot of our cases were conspiracies and as a result not petty theft but genuine investigation. This was right up my street.

I would spend eight hours in an off-licence with just my truncheon, two *Mars* bars and a can of coke waiting for an armed robber to enter the shop and plunder its takings from the safe. Initially in position from 10 am you would be on tenterhooks and every time the front door would bleep you would stay hidden behind the partition close to the safe. By eight o'clock in the evening and you would be going crazy with no food and no chance of getting replaced or relieved, only for some would be robber to enter armed with his sawn-off shotgun marching the owner to the safe, oblivious that we were behind him.

My partner and I would jump the guy, whacking him a couple of times managing to get the weapon off him. Seconds later the detectives would enter with hand guns to take control.

But it really was serious now with a murder every week for the first eight on Crime and after that nothing fazed you.

Stoke Newington was at times so demanding, but this was the new normal. There was no let up and so it was such a great grounding. The experiences were life lessons. I reasoned that if I could cope here then everywhere else would be fine.

Soon I was accepted as a Detective Constable, climbing again the ladder of experience within investigations and interviewing, followed by long periods of giving evidence at the Central Criminal Court ('Old Bailey') and then onto the famous grounds of Snaresbrook Crown Court and Inner London Crown Court. I was able to measure in my mind how far I had come already. All of it was a far cry from my woeful performance at Horseferry Road Magistrates.

Then the call came to see the Detective Chief Inspector. In those days you only saw him if you were in trouble so I feared the worst. And with it came the dreaded news that I was being transferred out of Stoke Newington and into the C.I.D at West End Central. I had no idea of the area or the Police Station, but I was assured that it would be good for me.

I was on the move again.

2

I was sad to leave friends within the job and friends outside of it, as well as many the publicans whom I had acquainted! I had now also moved out of the Section House and had rented a flat with a friend on a housing block on the Barking Road in Plaistow Canning Town in the East End of London – a stone's throw from the infamous West Ham at the Boleyn Ground at a time when the notorious Inter City thugs ruled the roost.

West End Central had it all for very different reasons.

We were located in the posh area of Savile Row and had the best-known streets in London like Oxford Street, Regent's Street, Shaftesbury Avenue and theatre land plus Tottenham Court Road, Soho, Carnaby Street, Mayfair, Chinatown and New Bond Street

Everyone flocked to these areas and during the day it was part of the tourist industry and places to be ticked off but at night a different clientele would walk the streets.

You had your pickpockets and robberies, but this was also the age of writing stolen cheques or using pinched credit cards. It was not uncommon to have some twenty cases per month. Large scale fights in clubs were the norm and were rarely straightforward as the victims would again come from all over London.

Actors and actresses flocked to the West End and were regulars in the bars and pubs around Soho after shows. Then there were those who took on the pleasures of the sex industry, your high-class prostitutes working in Mayfair, your well known hotels around Park Lane, your working girls in the seedy streets of Soho to the known 'Rent Boys' operating in side streets along with the transvestites operating out of bars and the massage parlours.

This was a million miles away from my experience of working at

Stoke Newington. Penzance was a world away.

I learned on my first day here in 1982 when I was introduced to the Commander of the Station who with his bark made it quite clear that as a detective you do not go to clubs. This was seen as the gateway to potential police corruption as had befallen Ken Drury, former Commander of the Flying Squad imprisoned after guesting in Cyprus under the hospitality of Soho porn baron James Humphreys but citing 'hunting Ronnie Biggs' as his alibi. My new boss would have no hesitation in putting me back to uniform if I did so. It was a stunning opening brief.

It was several days later when I met him again, entering the lift to go to my office on the first floor, confronted in his smart pin stripe suit and umbrella.

'Good morning, Sir,' I offered as he looked at me,

'Who are you?' he responded with his usual bark.

'D.C. James, Sir,' I replied. 'I'm new, just recently arrived here.'

His reply cut me dead.

'Well D.C James, walk the bloody stairs like everybody else. This is my lift,' he roared.

Welcome to West End Central.

I got stuck in immediately and my three years flew by as I signed up for everything that came in and exhausted my enquiries in the clubs hunting culprits of assaults – but yes, I did need to work those venues despite the advice.

I made a *deliberate* point of going to bars in the seedy part as well as the so-called up market ones, meeting people and understanding what all the fuss was about. I couldn't know at this point the bearing this would have on my future.

If truth be known I had a fantastic time working hard and playing hard. Its impact would come later.

I was fortunate that on a few occasions I was seconded to other Police Districts to assist in Murder investigations. Ironically this was a pleasant change from the work I was getting accustomed to. You soon become attuned whatever file sits in your in-tray.

Work was *never* dull. On one night shift, which itself could be a nightmare with three detectives covering the whole of the West End, I was at my desk doing some paperwork when a smartly dressed male entered the office, dressed in a black Crombie coat and the trusted pin stripe CIB2. He stated clearly there was nothing to worry about. They were conducting a search of the uniform lockers. This was known as the Rubber Heal Squad. Police officers were investigating police officers for that afore-mentioned corruption. I was not naïve to this despite the first day warning. Sadly, things had happened at Stoke Newington too.

'Anything expected of me?' I asked.

'No we are only searching the uniform lockers,' he replied. 'Just stay away from that area.'

Once they were out of sight I pondered and decided to call my senior officer. It was gone midnight but the officer appreciated the call.

Some officers were subsequently arrested and sent to prison. Regrettably, this did happen from time to time and an acceptance of what life was like. You were never quite sure whom you could trust even amongst your own. There was a lighter side too.

I was drinking in one of the pubs near Soho when the publican who knew me asked if I could spare a few minutes with this guy who wanted to know how to be a detective. I thought he was winding me up, so I stalled. He was an actor and playing exactly that part in the musical *'Blood Brothers'*!

I gave him some pointers and a few days later, he left an envelope for me by the bar with a couple of tickets for the show. From that moment on, we spoke regularly as he fine-tuned his character. In turn, I frequently met some of the cast including the singer Barbara Dickson. It wasn't quite dodgy favours on the normal Soho scale!

That aside my time in the West End was gradually building a rapport with licensees and customers. I regularly ran into the likes of Susan George and her husband the late Simon MacCorkindale, plus the *Hi-De-Hi!* cast and John Le Mesurier, famous principally for his role in *Dad's Army*. Fame or notoriety... one lesson shone through. Building rapport and establishing contacts was key.

By 1984 PC Yvonne Fletcher had been gunned down outside the Libyan Embassy in London as she 'manned' a protest there with around 30 other officers. Beyond that, there were no provocative circumstances. The consequences were colossal with the British S.A.S. storming their embassy eleven days later and the Prime Minister Margaret Thatcher severing ties with Libya.

Two years after, Thatcher supported the US President Ronald Reagan in allowing him to use British airbases to launch strikes against Libya. Nobody was held responsible for her murder.

I dealt with many cases that Yvonne was involved in. I had seen her just a couple of days before her death. The police conditions you because you will be associated with victims that have been murdered, died through natural causes, seriously assaulted with life-changing injuries and those who have been victims of sexual assaults. You show controlled empathy but emotionally you become blank as if you too are going through the motions. Personal sensitivity was viewed as a sign of weakness. A moment of reflection was done out of sight and away from prying eyes. She was in the wrong place at the wrong time. It was a phrase that would often accompany many police fatalities and injuries over the years.

Indeed, 1984 proved to me a massive year. Putting myself about meant that people would confide in me. But, at West End Central I was too busy to put my heart and soul into running informants and the information I was getting was classed as generally one-off, undermined by motives such as revenge, fear or removing some opposition. My limited intel was at least passed onto the Crime Squad which established some sort of personal credibility even if I could not nail a particular case alone.

In the same year, I was on my way to arrest a security guard working for a well-known store. The male lived in the East End and because it was alleged that he has stolen from his employer it was viewed as a serious offence. Theft from your place of work and breaking trust would be investigated by a detective.

'I am glad you have come,' he stated.

This was not what I was used to.

'It's only a couple of VHS Video Recorders,' I replied.

He took me to his spare bedroom, unlocked the door which could only be prised open slightly to peer in, and to my amazement it was stacked full of assorted property from records to recorders. It transpired that he had been stealing the property over a thirteen-year period.

'I cannot stop and I want it to end,' he stated.

Three trips with a Police Transit Van and a cell now packed high with the contents became an interest for everyone and meant that twelve months later at Knightsbridge Crown Court, he was charged with stealing items to the value of £46,000. He pleaded guilty and got four years behind bars.

In today's market you would be looking at a value nearer £250,000. It was a bizarre confession.

Around the same time, I also interviewed an elderly man for an allegation of stealing two figures from a very famous shop to the value of around £120.00. He was detained at the entrance.

The male was adamant he had not taken them and appeared a little confused. The store was intent on prosecuting and so he was charged with the theft. This man was a Polish Commander who had flown spitfires during the Second World War.

Later at Knightsbridge Crown Court he pleaded 'Not Guilty' and when questioned by his barrister he was asked if he had done it.

'No,' the man replied.

'Why have you pleaded not guilty to this charge?' the barrister asked.

The man somewhat shakily pointed towards me.

'The detective told me to,' he replied.

I showed no emotion but it did raise a rye smile from the Judge and some members of the jury.

He was found not guilty!

Working in the West End you found yourself in the most incredible areas. Even back then it was the playground of the rich and famous and from time to time our worlds merged. One day I found myself walking through the gardens of Berkeley Square in Mayfair on my way to some offices to meet an agency working on behalf of a well-known and renowned actress in Britain and Hollywood.

They handed me some letters from a fanatical fan who was now so excitable that they were making death threats. Mindful of the sensitivity of the matter, I assured them that I would deal with this appropriately.

I discovered that the fan had issues, but was severely disabled and so with common sense and a comforting chat, the letters ceased and I was able to bring the matter to a satisfactory conclusion. This variety of experiences was coming at me thick and fast and often in the seriousness of the work there was much to look back and laugh at.

In an interview situation I soon saw the extremes of the human mind. The most notable example was a slim male toned in a black tracksuit with his left hand heavily bandaged from a failed attempt to do a smash and grab of a jewellers in Oxford Street.

'Can I call you Ian?' he asked.

'I do not have a problem with that,' I replied.

'Do you mind if we stop the interview as I want to do 100 sit-ups? He asked.

'No problem, carry on,' I responded.

He then rose from the chair and proceeded to complete them followed by 50 press-ups. Having got up from the floor he then sat on the chair barely out of breath, let alone sweating.

I had never seen anything like it.

'Have you done any others?' I continued with the interview.

This was a pretty standard line of questioning. Few people just do one job.

'No, I have not done any more, but I did go into a hotel and placed some papers on a bed and set it alight,' he replied.

This guy was not right. He could turn at any moment.

He then went into full detail and calmly described its location and his rationale. I was taken aback by his transparency and felt obliged to terminate the interview and verify he was not spinning me a yarn.

I quickly established that he *was* telling the truth and that the very same night, a well-known hotel was set on fire and that six fire engines attended to put the blaze out and rescue occupants. Nobody had been injured. This was serious and he had confessed it all when I had only pulled him for theft. Arson with intent to danger life meant that it carried a life sentence.

As it was the weekend, 'C' District would have a covering Detective Inspector who would now oversee proceedings and we interviewed him together. Naturally, I warned my colleague about the exercise regime and it duly continued as he reeled off astonishing detail that only the actual arsonist could know. No surprise as to the result. He appeared at the Central Criminal Court and pleaded guilty to Arson with Intent to Danger life and was sent to an institution for an indefinite period. It was possibly the most extraordinary interview experience of my career – riddled with comedy and facilitated with ease.

And by now the experience of attending court was fine-tuned. As a detective you would be called upon to spend a week taking all the crime cases to the local magistrates at Marlborough Street just round the back of the London Palladium. How things had come full circle! One stipendiary sat at court was the very same person who had seen me flap through my first case at Horseferry Road Magistrates. He nodded and gave me a smile. I had learnt my lesson.

Of course, it was not all crime busting. There was an upside to the job in the many perks in the job. Everybody looked forward to attending Knightsbridge Crown Court, at the rear of London's iconic Harrods. Naturally at lunchtime you could go to the staff canteen at this renowned store and eat very well at staff prices! There was no greater incentive to go to court.

Three years had passed so quickly. My career was rising and Cornwall was a distant memory but for family. I was settled, originally living in the East End of London, then making the big step got onto the property ladder buying a two-bedroomed terrace house in Hornchurch, Essex, not far from the District line becoming a commuter to work for the first time with a daily journey of an hour. But I was now relishing the opportunity to return to areas that I considered better for me and of course renew my early friendships with experience on my side.

Indeed, I knew someone very well who had moved to Postings at Scotland Yard and through a friend of a friend I politely asked if I could be posted to 'K' District and a police station called Plaistow.

In the Metropolitan Police this defied the general rule that officers in specialist roles and the Criminal Investigation Department would only spend three years in any one place to prevent familiarity and corruption.

My friend joked that it would cost me an Italian meal and it proved to be the most important meal of my life. All these were experiences were taking me somewhere very specific.

An early marker as to what was ahead came at a bar in Soho, when a barman who I had known for a while leant over and stroked my tie suggestively, then proceeded to its top, meaning his hand was now close to my belt. I was being propositioned. I calmly took a step back, laughing it off, only to return the next day with my tie redone and the tip above my belly button. He saw the funny side and we remained friends. I was now truly understanding that much of this is played in the mind.

This was a new type of work altogether, at times having to enter the sex cinemas because a victim had their wallet stolen, therefore ordering the lights to be turned on while the movies still played leaving customers embarrassed with their trousers around their ankles whilst you look on the floor against a backdrop of smell of sweat, cigarettes and soggy carpets – and this was ten in the morning with it three times worse at night. You didn't get this in Cornwall!

My postings to Stoke Newington and West End Central were an incredible beginning enhancing my personal experiences and professional knowledge beyond my belief. It was time for a new direction. Two important people would in their own ways be instrumental in the subsequent path and journeys I would take.

But for me, there was one man who kept coming into my life whose influence straddled both those eras. It was his influence that took me to the dark places I arrived at. His instinct, his *own* story and desire to recruit that enabled both of us to redefine undercover work. One man had such a driving force without knowing so at the time that what I am about to tell you re-wrote police guidelines and legislation and re-shaped that whole anecdotal story-telling process by which fellow officers learn of what *really* went on.

That man is my late friend, dear George. I owe what happened next to him. In finding my own way from Penzance to Policeman, this is *our* unspoken truth.

This is my story.

3

It was not just George. *Two* significant people had in fact wandered into my life. Beyond my Dad's encouragement to head to London, these individuals were to be the single biggest factors in shaping the person that I would become.

Daily life in Plaistow Police Station in the heart of the East End Canning Town, Silvertown, North Woolwich and East Ham meant more murders, nasty police assaults and handling stolen goods alongside scrap metal thefts, lorry hijackings, drugs, armed robbers, pure crime families and inevitable football violence.

Some of the stabbings and glassings I attended were just ruthless unnecessary acts of revenge. It was a tense era to be a London policeman but I revelled in the prospect. This was reality with no pretence.

My new colleagues were all experienced detectives – amongst them a couple I had worked with when I was at Stoke Newington. So, I settled in well and began feeling my way around this vast area and naturally soon befriending publicans and its customers, knowing that over time information would be passed to me through these friendships.

The community threw up all types. Down at the King's Head pub in the heart of Canning Town, the boxing gym was located above, and when I entered I walked into Frank Bruno. We shook hands and engaged in banter with his trainer Jimmy Tibbs. You could see Jimmy was not a great lover of the law as we chatted from the gym benches watching this fighting machine go through his paces. That was typical of this patch. Mingling openly with those who deep down despised you became the norm.

Working the area, you would see hardcore criminals climbing the ladder like Pat Tate and Tony Tucker who would re-surface years later in high profile crimes most notably as victims in the atrocious Essex Boy murders of 1995. They were in my midst for the best part of a decade before they were shot dead with one other drug dealer in their Range Rover down a small farm track in the village of Rettendon.

Jack Whomes and Michael Steele received life sentences. It had been right under my nose.

The old gangsters and hardened criminals marked their territory, especially if you were new, They could smell a copper a mile away regardless of wearing a uniform but there remained an unofficial code in that if you were fair, then you were afforded some respect, but they still hated you either way.

We were encouraged to visit pubs that were not policed, meaning that you were going into *their* territory. They did not like it but you had to stand your ground and take the odd wise crack. It just had to be done.

The younger crooks were less respectful and more likely to stab you in the back. This was, in effect, a changing of the guard with a new breed emerging who wanted money now and wanted it at all costs. There were still no-go areas back then for some criminals who would not touch drugs for example, but were happy to cross a pavement with a gun and rob a bank or lift cash from a transit vehicle. It seems odd to write it now but all parties gave each other the relevant breathing space despite covert knowledge of what was going on. You knew where you stood.

And the young ones were indeed being played by the experienced criminals who would sit back, take less risks but all the spoils. In time, the greed of money meant that most did succumb to supplying the drug market.

There was genuine risk. On 6 October 1985, PC Keith Blakelock was murdered on duty. I knew Tottenham well. He had been patrolled with close to a dozen other officers after a black woman had died from a heart attack following a police search at her home. Keith fell when faced with a mob of close to 50 rioters and in the melee he received over 40 injuries from machetes and equivalents with one six-inch knife wound to his neck. At a time of unrest in many British cities, he became the first British policeman to die in a riot since 1833.

I was good friends and had worked with the officer who had led the search for the woman who had died. It didn't matter that it wasn't your area. You felt the affinity. Further unrest and violence in districts around London and other major cities followed, which then led to miscarriages of justice and acquittals of those persons charged with the policeman's murder and other officers for fabricating evidence. To this day the persons responsible for the murder of Keith Blakelock are still at large. It had turned really ugly for the first time.

I can still recall switching on the television news before going to work and watching in disbelief these events at Broadwater Farm and by now, I was being put increasingly on murder investigations.

I fell onto the radar of a man called John Grieve, who simply seemed to have experienced it all. I was keen to develop without being a career strategist and thankfully John saw the same in me. Generally, the force was very supportive in everything I did but in John I found somebody I could never fault. He was a knowledgeable and outstanding officer about whom nobody had a bad word to say. My instincts were correct that he was a good role model in that he ultimately became the Head of Anti-Terrorism in the Metropolitan Police.

At the time, John was the Detective Superintendent and the main lead investigator for murders on our district. He had specifically chosen me to do more murder work. He became the first colleague that I really didn't want to let down. So, apart from the very public plight of Keith Blakelock, my eyes and ears were now tuned in anyway.

Under him I was trusted to be an Exhibits Officer on several murder inquiries which at the time was seen as one of the most important roles of an investigation. A successful conviction could rest firmly on your shoulders. I was responsible for every item that came in as evidence to ensure the Crown Prosecution Services had uncontaminated material, some of which they may use or they may not. I was a regular at post-mortems and on other days I would be keeping safe for the prosecution a collection of exhibits ensuring that there was no break in the continuity of evidence.

Sometimes, this meant visiting crime scenes where normal life had since continued. My very first assignment on Exhibits was a murder and attempted murder involving a gang with armed robbery, where in the ensuing argument, one male killed another with a shotgun, then blasted a second man through the neck. Through incredible luck he had survived.

It was my job to go the house of the accused fully aware that he had a Rottweiler. When I arrived, I lifted open the letter box, and peered through to see the biggest head and pair of eyes looking at me. An absolute beast – and clearly not fed for a while. In the world of shotguns, it took an animal to throw me, and a team of dog handlers to extract it from the house. Its neglect was so poor that it later died. What did not throw me was eyeballing this violent assassin in court as I presented all of the physical evidence. By now, my court 'act' was well honed.

Of course, after a decade in London, I had met many people – friend and foe. I was a solid officer who had dipped into running informants. I would not say I was looking for the next challenge. I just simply enjoying my work, starting to gather good intelligence on armed robbers and also gaining invaluable knowledge of the mind of these criminals. Understanding the psychology of the corrupt and crooked was the next key stage in my development.

But by 1986 George was on my radar. It was a classic police relationship in that you might see him on a job and then perhaps a couple of months later you bump into each other again and through that a friendship and understanding slowly begin.

When I first met him in the C.I.D. office on the border of my district at Barking in Essex, I thought he looked an old bloke. His appearance would give you no clues as to what he did.

'That guy has a little of bottle,' a colleague chipped in when I hardly knew him at all.

'He did this job once and drove a vehicle. He showed a lot of bottle. He drove the robbers around.'

That was all I knew. George had some sort of legendary status but nobody really could explain why. I use the word 'legendary' in its traditional sense and not to play him as a hero. It literally was the way in the police that if somebody had excelled on a job which was essentially a need to know basis, their story would be told but only in scraps and often prone to embellishment. The less you actually knew other than that the job was big the further the tale spread. It was literally a legend.

He had a whiff of undercover about him in his demeanour but the extent of it really did not register until much later. All I actually could state as fact was that he was a CID officer and one of those people whom once you met, you never forgot and increasingly I would run into him more and more at court.

Working as a detective in the East End had been a great experience. My own Detective Inspector was about to recommend me to the 'Flying Squad' – a branch of the Met specifically investigating commercial robberies and preventing other serious crimes to which a firearm might be associated.

It would have been a fantastic opportunity to pursue but I did not give it a moment's thought as life had now intervened. That second key person had come into my world. I knew what I wanted and I was certain what came first. I was moving to Cleveland Police in the North East of England. I had fallen in love with Julie.

4

I had no idea what to expect and how different life might be up in the North East and they didn't really know what to make of me.

'Not everyone likes the Met,' my Detective Inspector told me before I left. 'Some people might think you are a cowboy.'

These proved very wise words and kept me focused. The very same Inspector had transferred back to his native Wales but, unable to settle, had returned to London several years earlier. At my exit interview with the Met, I had been deliberately balanced. It was made clear that the door was always open for a return. I was not about to slam it hard in their face by making flippant remarks.

Besides, I had loved it. In which other job could you find yourself entering a house in Canning Town to seize stolen goods only to find two young children (one in a nappy) sat on the sofa watching TV and next to them there was no parent or guardian to speak of – just the family horse! Now it was time to make new memories and prove myself again. Understandably so as the Met's reputation had not been great since around 1981.

Race and riot and a fear of prejudice had damaged outsiders' views of Scotland Yard. It was still very much an era pre-equality and pre-diversity. I knew of many people who had transferred to other forces but had ultimately gone back again. Outside of the city there was this dodgy reputation.

The media images of the trouble on the streets and division of skin colour and the constant footage of wielding truncheons defined both the public's and other forces' perception of the London bobby. Nor did the Miner's Strike – ugly scenes in the North East clearly showing drafted-in

Met Officers, easily identifiable by their different colour shirts.

By 1988 I was married to Julie and becoming accustomed to ways outside of London. Going back was not really in my thoughts. Being a police officer in uniform doesn't change in principle wherever you are. It is only the context that varies.

My introduction had been exactly as I anticipated. It was clear that what I had done previously counted for nothing.

I found myself working the front desk at Stockton-on-Tees Police Station. The contrast could not have been greater. Thankfully, I had provoked some curiosity and the Superintendent soon wandered in to talk to me.

He *had* read my file, and noticed that I had spent the majority of my service as a detective. Would I be wanting to re-visit that? I told him that I realised that I would have to prove myself, but yes, of course. With that, he then suggested being a Community Beat Officer for an area currently under-served?

Anything would be better than what I was doing on the desk but that annoyed my new supervision. I had only been there a short time and was now leaving the shift. That didn't help with perceptions of the man from the Met coming north.

Nine months as a beat bobby, getting to know the community on a housing estate, cultivating informants and dealing with criminal offences soon got me noticed. I was clearing up crimes and getting payments for informants, which wasn't the norm for uniform officers. For my new superiors, they were now learning fresh methods. For example, they were not used to accompanying me themselves to complete such payments.

My credibility was rising meaning I was then posted to the C.I.D. Feedback from the community leader for the housing estate was generous writing to thank me for my work but it was the fact that they also sought assurances that I would be replaced in my absence which told me that I had made a difference.

I was gradually winning people over and showing that I was not a cowboy and in a quiet way letting my work speak for itself. Occasionally I had to return to Plaistow to settle some outstanding cases. Much to *their* surprise, I was still in the North East and beginning to thrive. Finally, my patience and desire to be accepted meant that I rose again to the role of Detective Constable.

Once more, I cultivated informants, specialising in burglaries and the multi-million pound (even then) car theft industry. I also dealt with some sexual assaults and rapes and by 1991 I was urged to apply to the Regional

Crime Squad. From here, I found my niche that forms my story and with it, George re-emerged. And then, doors became ajar and stayed wide open for the rest of my career.

5

'You would be good in the undercover world,' I had been told. 'You've got a cockney accent.'

I had already lived in it of course… but as an officer known in that role to my subjects who were aware I was a cop as they traded me information. Could I immerse myself in it and pretend to be something I wasn't and assume an entirely new identity?

That was what was on offer.

Except merging into the undercover world as someone else was an undercover job in itself. From that one-off comment, fast forward to the canteen at New Scotland Yard. I am waiting to be collected for the start of my selection process, casually looking around me and noticing a few others wondering if they were also on the same path. Suddenly I hear a shout:

'Watcha Ian, how you doing?'

I looked up recognised a former colleague from Plaistow instantly wondering if he was here for the same.

The answer was no. He was just waiting for a mate.

I knew word would spread that he had seen me and that I was moving through the ranks.

Within minutes, an officer entered the canteen calling our names and we followed him into an office. There were ten of us in total and we were soon underway. And there he was. In the same room. You can't kid a kidder. I looked at my former colleague and we both burst out laughing!

First came the psychological assessments and a pre-interview, which we passed. The following day was the main interview, lasting an hour in a room deliberately devoid of windows and the heat on in every sense whilst three officers probed and assessed you across various scenarios and putting you under increasingly uncomfortable situations.

But I made it. I was in. And on the Regional Crime Squad, having completed my usual required surveillance courses, I then renewed some old acquaintances from my Met days who were more than happy to trade information again and that intelligence was invaluable getting into their minds and seeing crime through their own eyes as they would devise it such as planning a lorry hijack and then how to move the goods on and what to charge buyers rather than just being the cop at the end scenario. I was now in a much better position in terms of experience to interpret what they gave me. It was clear though that the best way to stop these people was to become them. So, I did.

By May 1992 I found myself attending an undercover training course. This was the key moment. George was there giving a presentation on child sex offenders and infiltrations. It changed everything. All that had gone before led here.

'That's what he does,' I thought.

Wow.

Very few people knew.

I learned that at the time he was probably the only person in the country doing this but it was so scarcely talked about that nobody was in a position to confirm or deny it. I repeat it was 1992. I found his work fascinating though it was very obvious that I was in the minority and many officers were not comfortable with taking on the kind of role he was alluding to. There was clearly a dark side. I did not occupy myself with the crime, more the methodology.

At any such training course there were two purposes: to explain what the work was and to recruit for it. I hadn't attended expecting to see him… let alone walk away with an entirely new career. The content of his session and his appearance were not advertised beforehand. George was on a hiding to nothing.

But this individual whom I had kept coming across on so many different occasions drew me in with his character and his jaw-dropping detail of his mystery world.

Afterwards he asked me where I had gone these last few years and I explained the move to Cleveland. It was as though we were meant to meet again and that presentation was specifically for me when plenty of others were in the room.

We chatted about 'old times' not that we had shared many, and our understanding grew. I asked him more about what he did and he picked up the vibe that I was interested. It was natural and spontaneous with neither of us knowing that we would have seen each other on the day. There was nothing orchestrated about us both being there.

And what he told me blew me away.

Then I met George again a few months later at a conference and had exactly the same chat except in greater detail. With even more undercover now under my belt I was intrigued.

I had so far spent my time buying counterfeit money, firearms, short and medium infiltrations, drugs and waded into £250,000 worth of stolen property and £500,000 stolen building society and bank cheques – forging was rife. This was pretty decent exhilarating work but it was a drop in the ocean compared to the potential that George was alluding to. I left the event with a lot to think about on many levels. But crucially, I was a supporter. Mentally, I was in.

There was a lot to weigh up before I could turn my life around, knowing that I would leave the house as one person and spend the day as another. It obviously could have enormous consequence at home and on the job. On a purely political level at the office there was still a suspicion of absence on unexplained work and that early London suspicion might come back to haunt.

'Don't be away from the office too much,' one senior officer had warned me previously as I began to travel frequently. 'I want a happy ship,' he said.

This kind of work would create jealousies. It could leave my career all over the place in that I was in unchartered waters because *was* no career path. Only George had this on his C.V.

Then there was the effect on a young family. What if my worlds merged and I found myself *in the role* through no fault of my own when I was in the house living a normal life? What about days out being interrupted or running another mobile that could go off at any moment?

This did not even consider what might happen if a job went wrong, my cover was blown, or I just could not cut off at night and leave the work behind. Let alone... my true address getting out there.

I had experienced a scare too.

The BBC investigative show *Panorama* had run an exposé on the use of informants by Custom Officers and police officers around this time. I was given about thirty minutes notice that the show would air and that my previous work would be alluded to. It really was the first moment where I crossed a line between police and personal emotions in that the thought of being identified would have a lasting impact for both the family and for the role.

I had worked very hard to get to this level and in a moment – in what the BBC felt was a coup for them in a show about Customs and Excise and the use of informants. I just got caught up in it but it was not specifically to do with me – I could lose it all. Before transmission, I even worried about how my accent would sound. That cockney which had been suggested as helpful for the role could bring me down if they chose not to distort it. They did indeed hide my face and change my voice but even the next day somebody approached Julie at the school gate and said that she was convinced she had seen me on the TV the night before.

Julie, as calm as ever, just laughed it off in disbelief.

It showed me a genuine concern about the blurring of my professional identities and real life.

The consensus within the high-ranking officers in the covert arena was that no damage had been done with the programme and my concerns were soon put to one side as I then began a four month infiltration with no adverse effect.

As a precautionary measure with one eye perhaps on what may lay ahead, I began to see a psychologist called Tom on a regular basis.

I expressed my concerns to George though they were not really worries for *me* personally.

'I've got a family,' I said. 'I don't know how I am going to deal with this.'

George, of course, understood because he was experienced and ahead of me in the process and whilst there was legitimate training to come, there could only be so much preparation and theory because as my story will show, there are some things that you cannot prepare for.

I weighed up the potential problems. The drive to do this work was eating away at me but equally I was quite capable of making a family decision as I had done when I left the Met.

Support from my bosses was also vital. They had to appreciate what lay ahead given that they might not understand the complex nature of it. Amongst my colleagues I would have to get used to explaining absences by saying 'it was just an assignment' knowing full well that the word 'just' was a massive understatement and always the give-away lie.

And as for Julie – well this could test us both but at this stage I didn't even fully know the nature of what *it* really was.

'Is it going to be a risk?' she asked as we both discussed what could have happened with the warning signs from *Panorama.*

She was brilliantly supportive.

'I don't want you bringing this home,' were her only words of caution and concern. And then she continued:

'But I do want to know what you're doing...what it is all about, so I can understand.'

And I would need that support. I had to have her backing if I was going to proceed. There were many undercover officers who went home to wives who knew absolutely nothing from even before the moment they became someone else. It was clear early on that Julie had to be aware. I broke that code by at least discussing what might be ahead and with that she gave me the green light to proceed.

It was clear that this was going to be a long road with no turning back where the rules would often re-define themselves. There was also the huge prospect of failure.

Julie had always be the one pushing me and encouraging me in my career. I had no strategy other than to be the best I could and hope that the work remained interesting. She understood what it all meant. She got it. And for the benefit of the family the sessions with Tom were to be my safety net to protect family life even though in the beginning we didn't have a lot to talk about.

I think we all knew we were investing in a future when one day we would...

6

In front of me in a private room at Scotland Yard images were laid out. Pictures upon pictures of nudity, of depravity and of innocence lost. One such still would be enough to cause you to make an early exit and re-consider your decision to say yes.

I didn't have that option. I had hours of this stuff in front of me. Day after day. Often, on my own. We deliberately chose a sterile empty office in London. This was obviously not something I could look at on the train or leave lying around on the kitchen table at home.

I would pick up the photo and then put it down. Then I would move on to the next one. I was, of course, aware this stuff was out there even though it was 1992 and the Internet hadn't yet given this material a home. We were still some years away from cyberspace changing all our lives. I suppose I knew that there were vast quantities of it too. I now had to find a method to deal with it.

I had learnt to step back from my emotions and develop a poker face whilst doing my undercover work, but this was different. I was preparing for no face at all. I had begun the process of de-sensitising me – of conditioning myself to a norm of no reaction at all.

The criminals that I would be dealing with in the future looked at these kinds of images all day long. These were standard to them. I had to learn not to react or be shocked and move past even a wince towards developing a smile of pleasure at what I was seeing.

There was no time frame to perfect this. I just had to keep going over image after image knowing that one day I would be in a room with the sick and depraved and would have to become one too. I had to learn no reaction and then a positive reaction. The need to work on my own facial impressions akin to what *they* would use was paramount. I was essentially stripping back the person I was, just for the role.

This was a massive step for me because as a human being you are doing something unnatural. For the avoidance of doubt, I have no interest in a sexual way and so I am acting.

I am taking the role of undercover officer to an unprecedented level.

The importance of this particular aspect of training is vital. In a flash a picture could be in front of you. All eyes are on you. One false reaction and you put the operation and more importantly, the child at risk.

I was largely self-taught. George encouraged me and shared experience in training but it was always going to be about my character and my traits because I could be in that room with these monsters and it was highly likely that it would be just me from the police. I had to find my own way despite the excellent support George was giving me.

That method that manifested itself was based on one fundamental belief. If I learnt to look past, almost through, the image from the moment it was placed in front of me, then I would be devoid of any polarising reaction. It seemed for me the only way.

But that was just the beginning.

Once I was comfortable with my reactions, I then had to learn to talk about the pictures and decide in my own mind what *I* liked. Once you have your sex, age and preference in your mind then you cannot flip to something else. Consistency in your character was everything. I wasn't talking about arms or cars or drugs any more. This was a new breed of criminal who was passionate about a human being and believed they had justification for their sexual love of a child. This, of course, was brand new territory.

If I decided that I was particularly fond of a child in the seven to twelve age group and the sex of that child, then I had to stick to that and remember in the days ahead what I had said on day one. If I said I disliked an image I needed to recall if it was because the child was plump, or their eyes or hair were not my type. I would have to show enthusiasm at some point whilst remaining convincing.

Infiltration into their world would require huge skill. Recall would be the decisive factor in staying credible and therefore within their company.

There was a lot that I had to consider across many aspects. I studied previous admissions and disclosures from past victims. At the back of mind was the fact that if we had any success at all, the legislation was still very archaic and also that we could not be accused in court of incitement. We could not have been seen to have led anyone towards crime. They had to take us there. You read this in the context of today. I was operating in a grey area over a quarter of a century ago.

The task in hand therefore meant assuming an identity and carrying that off devoid of reaction, plus infiltration of individuals or groups, and crucially so, preserving and not contaminating evidence with the end goal of perhaps a year or so down the line being able to present a case in court under very old and vague laws.

In short, I was the actor, the technician and the policeman. And then at home, I was the husband and the father.

But I was committed.

In my heart, my mind was moving towards this new role but in 1994 there was no certainty that it would be permanent or the resource would sustain it. We didn't know what dangers the Internet would soon bring. George told me that there were now just five of us including me in the country working in this field.

But he stressed one thing which I never lost sight of:

'If you can stop one person than you have done more than anyone. It's all about the child.'

Measuring success and therefore the program continuing, was as simple and complicated as that. But the brief was clear even if the process would be painstaking.

Save one child. It's all about the child.

7

One day the phone was going to ring and all theory would become a reality – of sorts.

'I know you can do this,' I remembered George saying after the seminar. 'There will be dark days.'

Until I actually began, none of us would really know how black, although George had experience and was all too aware.

I flitted back between London, the Home Counties and the North East, forever running informants and still buying stolen stuff in the role of my normal undercover work. I would never undermine that important police work but I had a taste of what was to come and it became very difficult to not see that the new assignment was where a lot of mental energies were heading.

George remained on the level, always supportive and offering fresh insight.

He took me back to some of those places in Soho that I had already frequented in my previous roles. Many were not for the faint-hearted.

You would find two people in a toilet or plenty around a cubicle. These were danger signs. Upstairs, you would often have to walk across a catwalk to the bar knowing all eyes were on you and then wait for someone to pick their moment before propositioning you and pinching your bottom.

George would play the scenario in the interests of training.

'You're nice,' an 'admirer' would say.

'I'm with somebody,' I would answer.

'No, he's not.' George would counter, forcing me to engage.

This was an important technique because at some point in the future I would probably be in a gay bar and need to learn the skill of letting down gently somebody whom I needed to befriend, knowing that in effect they had eyes on younger prospects. Learning to go through the motions to the end game was key.

Even 'you're not my type' was a difficult rebuff because it essentially provoked the next question 'well, what is your type?' and that is where the recall comes in.

That fixed position of saying that I liked seven to twelve years should never alter. You did not chop and change every time you were in a new scenario within the operation. Keep your story simple and make it consistent. The one important factor was to research your target and work with their sexual ages of interests. Use the same drill and be wary of the one unknown ahead – that you could encounter individuals in more than one set of scenarios. Certain players could wander into your story several times at different stages. You never knew where a network began and ended. Keep it basic and make it consistent.

George and I talked about breaking down barriers with potential targets over a sustained period of time beyond that initial meeting where you might attempt to infiltrate. We were aware of two points.

Firstly, you *could* say something that could knock an operation back three months. Many of these people we were about to deal with had control and ego issues.

Secondly, pick a hobby. It was a common trait from previous case files that these individuals normally had a very specific interest outside of children.

Buses, trains, canal boats – whatever it was, they liked to see themselves as experts in something. Listen to them and feed that self-esteem. Find your own hobby too that was as close to a real you and that might interest them. You had to have natural conversation. It was a mistake to think that they all did was talk about children.

In fact, the opposite was often true. I learned early that paedophiles despised that very word along with 'grooming'.

These were terms that authorities had imposed on society and did not represent them in their own eyes. They were victims of language designed to mis-portray them. They would never use such words.

If anything, they would counter by saying that in fact they loved children. They *did* have their own code words too. Children were spring chickens.

Importantly, it was paramount that I had an understanding of what the paedophile was and how they used their skills to identify locations that attracted children. How they would blend in and disappear within the crowd and yet be within touching distance of their prey.

I had to understand that walking through a park with the attractions of the duck pond feeding the ducks with bread would be crowded with children of all ages and, just as importantly, a parent. To interact simply using bread from a carrier bag was an opportunity to engage with child and parent. The parent was the key to the child.

Your retail parks cater for everybody, but those who design such centres would not have bargained for the predator who wants to get close to a child who will be oblivious to its surroundings when playing a XBox game, machines or the amusements. The predator wants to get close even if it is to smell the innocence, and that excites them.

He stalks the child and remains undercover, using natural surroundings like communal eating areas and coffee shops avoiding alerting the attention of security.

Retail parks, beaches, parks, amusements, arcades, shopping malls, eating areas (fast food), indoor activities, leisure pools, sports centres and tourist attractions all provide a purpose for the predator to lurk and engage. I needed to educate myself so I was not out of place or a novice.

I needed to understand how the predator works the parent to work the child. Two completely different kill sets. Innocently befriending the adult offering help or friendship to get to the child then working the minor so that if he or she ever reported back to the parent, the adult had already achieved a level of trust so the child would be doubted.

Crucially too, George told me that they were working to change the legislation but it was a slow process. In time, this kind of work would be better supported but that time was still a long way off. The defining Sexual Offences Act did not arrive until 2003, the best part of a decade on from when our work began. Until then, all our potential investigations would be defined by the 1956 Sexual Offences Act and staggeringly, The 1824 Vagrancy Act.

In relation to the task ahead the former covered rape, incest, assaults, abduction, prostitutions, indecency between men and essentially intercourse with girls under thirteen or girls between thirteen and sixteen.

Paraphrasing, it did not get much broader or more specific than that. For the latter, don't even ask. The main parameters in which I would work revolved around laws on people 'lodging in a barn or an outhouse' (also a coach-house, stable, near a canal or adjacent to a highway) and people who were deemed rogues and vagabonds.

It was as bland and archaic as that.

We were heading into a new era, ahead of the Internet but held back by a judicial system that still thought Dick Turpin was out there. Realistically the world *did* work like that. Laws got passed in response to situations that have already happened.

It often takes looking back at a tragedy and the obvious flaws in the process to make new laws that banish these forever. We couldn't really know in 1994 what lay ahead with grooming online but I do not need hindsight to tell me that the offences were already there. It was only the methodology and playing field of the predator that changed with time.

It did not hold me back in my belief for the work. I liked George a lot so the personal investment was a fait accompli plus I knew this really was happening and in essence our work would be the proof that the laws had to be changed so I could not allow that to be a distraction. I had to work with what we had for now and just be clear about the evidence being placed into the law of that day.

Whilst time on a job would become experience that no training could match, George constantly re-iterated principles that never left.

'You cannot allow anything to happen to even one child,' he had said repeatedly. 'It's all about the child.'

That meant even if I was so close to Mr Big that I had realistically had to somehow 'sacrifice' a child for the greater good to expose a wider network then that was never ever to be an option.

We spoke on the phone. We met in person. We had a duty of care to each other. As time went on the five of us became a family within the undercover world. I knew that first job was coming. Theory would soon become reality.

I drilled myself to the principles of this new role.

Work on your own back story and make your hobby good as a source of common interest that shares conversation; view the images in a controlled environment and be comfortable with them – expand that comfort to feigned joy in discussion; learn to talk in graphic sexual language without faltering – this was their mother tongue.

Next, in a one on one scenario avoid their advances without being compromised. Be able to corroborate everything you say in the moment *and* in the months ahead. See danger. Understand the capability of the technology you were carrying or often, wearing.

Be mindful of the wild card – what if by chance a suspect is identified in broad daylight by someone else he had tried or indeed had sex with? Take care in case of assault from others; avoid your own photo being taken for the unknown location of where it may end up. Prepare yourself that you will be called an undercover journalist at some point. Overcome fear of failure – not every job will be a hit. Learn how to back it all up for the moment justice calls in the future.

Be wary of location – you have no idea where these people may take you. You could be in a homeless centre as they seek free meals. Don't commit yourself into the unknown. Sexual aggression may fall on your lap – become accustomed to gay bars.

Deal with the pressure. Deal with the pressure of dealing with the pressure.

And then do these drills all over again.

And this was before it began. But it was about to.

I couldn't talk about it to anyone. Except George a little, and Tom, the psychologist who was now well in place and had a lot of experience of dealing with victims. I was not in that category yet, but the risks were clear ahead. His main work with me was putting the hours in early and he was excellent at making sure I did not contaminate my home life by bringing material or work home.

The important issue was always keeping Julie in the loop, knowing and appreciating what and why I was doing this work.

This was all in theory of course. Training versus reality.

Suddenly it was game on.

It was now real.

I had to go to Wales.

8

Sex tourism was the word.

People would go abroad and the purpose of the holiday was to buy underage sex. It was a concept that was alien to me but it was not a new thing.

But now it was our thing. In my second year of training and after many sessions with the councillor, it was live. It had taken that long.

I was always aware that prep for a job could come become reality at a moment's notice but there is no doubt that the heart races when the scenario begins.

The first reference point in everything that I had absorbed in the last two years was simple. I had only one chance to make a first impression. This would always be true.

Intel had suggested that I was dealing with a group of men between 40 and 60 – probably reasonably affluent – and they had a liking for abroad. Someone call Billy was organising sex trips away. My job was to see if he was facilitating operations in Thailand. This immediately drew one conclusion – that whatever they got up to here at home was just the start of it. If we could show their desire was to journey to other countries with a different culture and even more relaxed legislation than our antique set of laws then clearly we were casting the net far. If the perception was that they could get away with it overseas, the roots of it must be here. I felt sure that overseas meant safety to them but at home they couldn't go that long in between trips without something similar and there must have been detail in how they became a group in the UK. It was potentially a double sting – home and abroad.

After a couple of planning meetings and clearance to proceed from the Assistant Chief Constable, we had the green light.

We knew these guys were smart, most likely quite influential and unchallenged in the community. Often married too. This was not uncommon. We, and *they* both knew there were a few journalists sniffing around at this time. If we could avoid that stigma, their surroundings looked as though we could enter their world.

It was time to begin.

George and I were working together. This was not planned but possibly inevitable and perhaps wise on the first 'real' job. Nobody could really know how things would go beyond the fact that we were both skilled in undercover. We knew each other well enough to know in the field when the moment arrived and who should take the lead.

This would be different though. We were dealing with people who were in denial, whom our training told us detested those words 'paedophile' or 'grooming', designed to belittle and stigmatise. They weren't cruel to children. I remembered that I had read that time and time again in previous cases that they believed they loved them. They often saw themselves as untouchable and, high on security, this could take months.

Penetrating a group would require all the skills of patience and communication that we had honed over the years.

We dressed nondescript. It was important to appear normal. I needed to be comfortable too as Julie had carefully sewn clothing in a way that I could hide recording equipment without appearing awkward.

Our information said they liked their restaurants and we had established what seemed to be one of their favourites out in the countryside and when given the nod that they were settled and eating, pulled up in a cab around 40 minutes after they did.

It was very difficult not to nudge each other and say in hushed tones 'that's them' when we arrived – except of course, we were highly trained not to. The restaurant was both busy and tightly packed. That could have made the night tricky in terms of getting close to them and indeed making sure that their voices were clearly isolated against the background noise on the tape we were recording on but it also worked to our advantage in that we were eventually seated next to them so the inevitability of cross-table conversation was a given. We had no control over this but clearly it was ideal.

But timing was everything – the moment to enter their conversation had to be seized without being planned. So, George and I made a conscious decision not to be too loud yet obviously they could have eyes and ears on us intermittently as you do in a tight dining area.

From time to time, we would look their way with the principal purpose of isolating a weak individual in our mind within the group. Who was dominating the conversation? Were any vulnerable and subservient to others? These collectives often had an unspoken hierarchy.

We knew one of them was probably the leader. 'David' liked to talk a lot. It might be him. George and I probably just looked like two gay men out for a meal.

Despite my experience and knowing to be patient, I felt the pressure to engage. At times it was agonising. They were only two to three feet away. Your mind splits into parallel train tracks – one concentrating on the normality of George ordering a steak; the other honing on tone, innuendo, specific phrases or topics of conversation that might be an entry point at pauses in their dialogue.

One eye was always on a metaphorical clock. That means that they had started before us and would leave accordingly. It could be 9 pm or 10 pm but you judged the time by only two factors. How much battery time would you be getting through in the technology, *and* if they started to order desserts then it was probably too late to make a move.

And that move had to be subtle – very much without drama. A toilet break or a drinks order seemed the obvious ins right from the outset. I too would need a strategic loo visit to change the tapes without arousing suspicion in the way I walked, the length of my absence, or the nature of what I was doing. And if we managed to engage, the whole purpose was not for now. It was to plant an opportunity to meet again. We had our cover story ready to go.

We knew too that our accents stood out. There was a decent chance that could get us an opening into the conversation.

Then the moment came. They took their natural break leaving their table relatively empty but for one of the group.

'It's nice here,' I half said to George and half said in their direction without turning fully round.

Then he bit.

'Are you from round here?' a softly spoken Welsh accent engaged.

This was it.

I turned, told him that we were from London and could see he looked a spare part while his mates relieved themselves or re-fuelled.

'We are sightseeing, looking for properties,' I replied without wanting to sound dismissive or flippant.

I could see he was less mobile than the others so I used my communication skills instantly to build a bond knowing that I would likely be cut off soon on the others' return.

'My friend here has his ailments,' I began, explaining that really I was looking to buy on his behalf. 'We have come a long way but I hope it is worthwhile.'

I put three things out in a couple of short sentences. We might be gay. We needed property. George and he had common ground.

There was reason to engage.

As the others came back, I continued so that we became part of each other's conversation.

'Look at him,' I gestured to George trying to keep the dialogue superficial but good-humoured. 'He's had that massive big steak.'

And George was not a big eater.

'Are you from the area or passing through?' another asked as they sat down again.

It was good chance to underline the point and practise in sticking to the script. Stay in character and stay true to the answers. Avoid embellishment and do not be sucked into inventing a new answer for a new person. Add to the detail but don't change it.

'We've got money and we don't want to lose it,' I tried to appeal to their wealthy lifestyle. 'I will be looking to get up here once a month until we find the right thing.'

I gave them new carrots. I was one of *them*. I had the cash. Also – I would be back. There was a chance we could meet again. Plus, I was sending them a message according to the profiling that I had learned about this type of person. I was asking for an expert to show me the way.

They revealed little but were relaxed and took the bait.

'Be careful,' one piped up. 'The estate agents will rip you off.'

I told them that had been my fear.

'Here's my number,' I offered 'Stephen' trying to ensure that second meeting. 'I am looking to come back next week and if you don't mind, I would love to pick your brains.'

I gave them plenty of opportunity to knock me back but somehow this appealed to their ego. They *were* true to type.

'Let me know if you are definitely coming up,' offered the slightly less mobile gentleman with whom we had made the initial contact. 'I would love to meet.'

And it really was that simple on the night – except of course that the intelligence had given us the perfect window and that research, training and years on the job made it seem so easy.

Timing, common traits with the targets and the key desire to build a relationship patiently knowing that you could be months from the end game had been key.

'That went really well,' George said after as they left whilst we remained.

You wouldn't take any chances in a situation like that by hastening your own exit. Your evening had to be seen to continue as they went on their way. But George was right and even though this was new territory, it probably was textbook. There is the variable that some people just will not take to you – that happens, and I hated failure – and they had every reason to disengage with us given the years they had been so secretive together. By playing one and knowing exactly which buttons to press, we had an in.

At the debrief that night, our two colleagues shadowing us agreed that it could not have gone any smoother. It was important too to do the admin as soon as possible after the job. Some dialogue would not have been picked up by the tape and I needed to make notes for the cold light of day for whenever this might come to fruition.

But I was secretly ecstatic, comfortable with my style in not having tried to be something I wasn't.

George and I agreed that the only proof of whether this had been a success would be if he did indeed call me.

The following Sunday, Stephen did ring.

9

This of course broke the rules. Everything I had talked about with Tom the psychologist and all the concerns that Julie had about work not entering the house fell at the first hurdle. We were learning as we went.

On this occasion, it was unavoidable as my 'dirty' phone beeped into action. The conversation was short and uneventful – this time. I couldn't know if in the future this line would be crossed either again or regularly. These types of characters were unlikely to call me as though they operated 9 to 5 but equally I couldn't *not* answer.

Since the restaurant, my gut feeling was that we had picked the right guy in the group. There was absolutely no guarantee he would remember or have the desire to phone me. True to his word he becalmed my Sunday that had been spent flitting in my mind between the family and the anxious hope that he might.

That nervous energy is difficult to hide during the day, as is the sheer elation at something so simple that he had rung. It told you that you were good at your job and that you had succeeded so far. They had no issues of trust.

Taking the call at home at the weekend presented multiple issues beyond the contamination of family time.

It had been drilled into me that these individuals might turn around at some point in the future and say 'remind me how we met again'. Much of their dialogue was a test. I couldn't be thrown off guard by allowing conversations to interrupt home life to the degree that it might damage my recall going forward. I had to remember every detail, always.

Equally, a dog barking, a milkman smashing a bottle, a friendly neighbour, a car tooting in the area you describe to them as home or a baby crying that in the moment that you pass off as your sister's children when later you are exposed as not having seen your sister in years…all of these normal aspects of life are trouble. No flippant made up excuse to get you out of that particular hole could be justified. It could expose you later.

My own children were four and six at the time. They were very likely to step on a toy or shout Dad at any moment I could be on the phone. The controlled sterilised room in which I trained betrayed the randomness of home life. There were too many wild cards to be taking even a simple call at home.

Julie knew that Stephen might ring. We both knew he might not phone at all. At this stage there was no real know-how as to how the angst at a no-show might affect my behaviour.

When the call came, my instinct was to exit the house. I made for my garage and closed the door, but I wanted it out of the house.

'I might lose you,' I pre-empted any problem. 'The signal is very dodgy around here.'

The good thing about that line is that in time, he might get used to me saying it and it was a totally acceptable line to deliver. It always gave me an excuse, an opt-out and a reason for brevity.

'I will probably be there around Wednesday or Thursday,' I offered.

My language was deliberately specific in its vagueness. Eight words that included an adverb of doubt and two choices of days cast my net far and gave me the chance to backtrack and re-schedule if he didn't like those options. It also gave me the opportunity to re-confirm to ensure no journey was wasted. This was how calculated you had to be to always ensure you moved to the next base.

And, of course, I needed to be doubly mindful of what I was saying in that I had no control in the home environment and that meant I was not recording. I couldn't sit there all day ready to tape whilst still largely keeping much of my work from my family and not knowing if indeed he would call.

So, as I stood there in the field, I knew I had to make notes straight away when I had finished because the next time we would meet I would have to re-run the phone conversation with him to show for the record that he had placed that call and I had not coerced him. This was a very long game of chess, played very, very slowly.

Equally, it was important to show respect in the calls. I began to use phrases, which would become the mainstay of my armoury like 'I really appreciate it if you give some guidance' or 'I would be grateful if you could give us a steer'. Appearing vulnerable in knowledge added to a wider picture of the same. Play to the expert.

I also had been told that many of the characters that I would be dealing with succumbed to the trait of wanting something for nothing and this often applied to transport. I knew with Stephen's mobility limited and restricting his social life, I could make him pleased to see me.

'What day is best for you?' I asked having put my own days on the table ensuring there was such a pool of availability that we would definitely be on.

I had just one final drill to run. I made him read his number back to me as he had only mine to this point.

I concluded by saying I would confirm and ended the call buzzing that the job seemed on. I think my colleagues would always say my temperament was pretty even but when a contact connects then inside you want to punch the sky with joy – not because you are over-zealous and love the chase but because you know you have done your job properly.

Then when you are finished, you call it in, the office takes his number to check him out and you call the Superintendent to ask his opinion before you get a yes. In the meantime, your part is done for now while others carry out a risk assessment and check his address and phone records.

And all the while I was still running informants and assisting in operational cases back in Teesside leaving nobody any the wiser internally outside the circle of trust that anything had changed.

Either way, I knew I was going back to Wales. And the man I knew as Stephen.

10

The reality is I was beginning to run more than a double life. I had £40,000 worth of cannabis coming into the country from the ports from a 'tip off' from one of my informants.

The best part of three years' worth of surveillance by specialist police units meant that security cash in transit vans was also on my remit as a result of some of my informants supplying snippets of information; the armed robbers regularly following them to see if they made any sudden changes in pick up times or if their likely raid was near vulnerable locations that could isolate guards doing their drops, together with potential escape routes they might use. It was routine but important work. Armed robbery was a constant despite major cities now introducing CCTV designed to counter act potential terrorism. The hardened criminal was still wanting to cross the pavement with firearms and intent to steal.

But the new job was occupying my mind and George, for the purposes of our cover story and also because it was fact, was back in London. Much of the pre-work had been done for me.

There was not an estate agent in Wales whose brochure I hadn't seen. I called Stephen back on the Tuesday and he was keen. The now familiar manly voice would answer, only to slip into a feminine overtone when comfortable. I kept my options open on the time of my arrival, saying I could overrun with the agents when in fact I was just building in the reality of traffic etc. I left him in no doubt that I was coming. I was just preparing for life getting in the way.

I booked a hotel in a neighbouring town. I kept a log too of what I was wearing so I didn't move from one job to another and compromise myself.

My fake Achilles' heel would always be that I pretended to know nothing about mobiles and computers and I would need their assistance and in this world that would help me get a long way. In the on-going bid to recall what has gone before, the office would always give me last minute intel. The goal would never change – set up the next meeting.

On this, the second meeting, I already found myself at Stephen's house. 'Where would you like me to sit?' I asked, almost obedient from the word go. He had his own favourite chair, from which I imagine he had often held court.

We chewed the fat on everything. You had to become a specialist in small talk. 'I think this might appeal to me but I am not sure about George.' I re-iterated my reason for being there and the insinuation of a relationship as I showed him brochures.

I had come armed with correspondence. There was no way we would run out of conversation.

'What are you thinking of doing with it?' he would answer.

I would reply 'renting' as we went through the motions of our pretence.

'I'd like a little bit of a garden but George is not bothered.' I was already setting out my stance of our opposing views as if to emphasise the point that he Stephen was the expert and I was asking for help and that George and I might never come to an agreement. I was buying all the time I needed.

Décor gives clues. His living room was meticulous. It felt like he had a cleaner. His china tea set stood out. I spied a black and white picture of a lad in his teens and asked politely who he was only to be told he had died of an overdose. That might not have been the entire story or the genuine answer.

I never saw Stephen's bedroom.

I was conscious of the fact that I could never give false promises to him. He was younger than me but there was the silent whisper of George to keep him at bay. My sole aim was to see where he sat within the group and to use him as a reference to get to others. If I built a solid one to one with him, then when I befriended the others, I hoped he would endorse me and say I was fine.

And so began five months of travelling down to Wales and back, trying to work the relationship. On that second visit, he told me that he had hosted a lot of parties. This is what I came to recognise as slowly edging towards that middle ground where one of us might put something definite on the table.

A lot of his friends had come and gone in life – he too had seen better days. Badly overweight and often in ill-fitting jogging pants, I had no empathy for him as a human being and I rejected his advances but I had to try to show that respect needed, using phrases of trust like 'If I can be a little bit open with you'.

The whiff of the promiscuity of parties and the younger individuals' photos still didn't meet any hard evidence that he was abusing boys. I couldn't take him there unless he led the way. Again, I was always mindful of where the evidence might sit in 18 months.

The cagey, one step forward-two steps back conversation almost brought us to the suggestion that George and I might be invited to these infamous parties but never quite got us there.

Attending too could open many doors for us but was a massive risk because of the unknown. You could not do the intel on people not yet on the radar who may be on a guest list to a party that you would never see.

One of the rules remained to be cautious regardless of where it might take you and if you had to drop that opportunity to proceed with risk, you did. And this, alongside the knowledge that they might always question every encounter with you, was never better demonstrated than with one very distant person within the group who had served in the Forces.

It was a test. He was throwing a pebble across the ocean.

We had begun to put the word out that we were thinking of going to Thailand. That is where the intelligence led us. I had asked Stephen for advice privately. There was little more in our explanation than it was the kind of place you didn't – you know – get caught. That was our biggest card, indicating what we were after though they give little back often talking in riddles.

Stephen had previously endorsed me when I specifically went to visit this former Sergeant Major at his own house for more information and he virtually blanked me, not giving an inch even though he knew why I was there and even though Stephen had cleared me, leaving me having to go back and ask why, only to be told that the guy had already called and had been assured it was all fine. He told me that he had never met me before even though he had been at the restaurant with us on the first occasion!

'He's suspicious,' Stephen pacified. 'That's the way he it is.'

I went to see him about going to Thailand but *specifically* told him I was worried about getting caught. One individual had been arrested there recently for sex with a boy when historically the feeling was you would be fine. For that reason, his guard momentarily had gone up.

When it was safe to revisit the subject, the group later passed the arrest off as nothing to do with under age activity at all but merely a corruption issue in that part of the world. It diverted the story as though they had time to think it through when they knew otherwise. And so did I. It avoided them having to condemn a fellow paedophile and use that very word itself. The detained had done nothing wrong and nor did they – they adored children without alluding to anything beyond. The system was corrupt. That was the only explanation.

It showed that working a group was hard and that one entrance point to the ring still meant that every time you re-entered you have to pass new tests and fresh scrutiny and it was the person in the services who took this to a new level. He played the military man with me.

There was always this almost fictional half-conversation that the big man from Thailand was on his way over. They kept alluding to their contact. It proved nothing except their connections did lie there. They played with it, they tossed it around and then left it hanging – this notion that above them was this man they aspired to. They would mention him and then drop it. They controlled the speed of the revelation only for one day at the house of an associate of the group, to become real.

Suddenly they wanted a photo to send him. They upped the stakes.

This was a problem on so many levels. I had conditioned myself to looking at indecent images in training. I worked tirelessly to enact no reaction or a fake positive reaction. I hadn't considered that my own image might suddenly be snapped and sent spiralling out of control to an individual or a group on the other side of the world where the legislation was even worse than ours in that in was virtually non-existent and I could not know where that picture might end up in the short-term or further down the line. In the same breath, I couldn't really feign an opt-out. I could protest that I was shy and didn't like having my picture taken but to progress with these guys, I was left with no choice. Any flicker of doubt or protest in the moment would cut me adrift let alone what might happen with the picture. I never saw that associate again. This was sloppy that an unknown person had snuck under the radar and it was beyond our control.

Then things got worse.

11

George and I were now eating regularly with them. We had a level of acceptance but it still contained obstacles. Time had passed and I waited for the desserts to be ordered before I made my routine trip to the toilet to change the tapes. I knew I always had a small window. The need to be clinical and calm was paramount.

I would mark the tape in a cubicle so that I had some sort of idea which was which on playback. I would number the fresh one going in.

I was always clock watching. How long was realistic to be at the toilet? Especially if you actually needed to go too. I couldn't be back there in the gents a few minutes time if I actually needed to pay a visit.

And when I returned to the table I had to be confident in my poise. The speed of the changeover could not leave me short by having something hanging out or equipment not quite being settled inside what I was wearing.

But when I came back to the table, something *didn't* feel right. I had a bad feeling in my stomach. It was nothing to do with the group or the photo nor the scenario that we were hoping would unfold.

I had dropped a clanger.

The job had so many aspects to it all needing care and attention at the same time but equipment couldn't embarrass you. I had to make my excuses and feign a return to the toilets.

When I said I had a bad feeling in my stomach that also became my excuse for a second dash to the loo in a matter of moments. My metaphorical explanation was a whole lot worse.

I had left the tapes on top of the urinal.

This is where that ticking clock that can both drag and count down suddenly catapults itself into fast forward spinning round like a timepiece out of control. They were my priority now as I retraced my eye line back to the washrooms visualising if anyone had entered as I left.

Did my own exit from the table look convincing? Would anybody accompany me to see if I was alright? What if a member of the public picked up the tapes or toyed with me as I tried to get them back?

And then I had to bury them in my body which again would take time. Little fazed me because despite the potential risky nature of our work, we always set up scenarios where we had as much control as possible. Going to their party was therefore not an option. Having that photo taken was a wild card for which I was not prepared and could not to this day find a decent opt out from. Letting yourself down because you were so relaxed in the role was potentially unforgivable if you blew the contact. And of course, unless somebody grabbed the tapes before me – which they didn't – you still couldn't know if your behaviour seemed atypical and the problem was that you might never know but it could sit there as an undercurrent into the foreseeable future.

I had to play dumb – as if food poisoned.

Eventually after ten minutes or so after I sat back down, George asked if I was OK.

'I am now,' I replied.

And I meant that both acting and in the belief that I thought I might have got away with it and if I could leave him doubting then I would probably be fine.

I had to assume that there was no lasting damage in the group. Outside of Stephen, they were so guarded that you couldn't really know but until told otherwise I had to proceed and whilst everyone on Ops was concerned about the photo, the only plus that came out of it was that the much-mooted visit from the man in Thailand materialised.

He really did exist.

I felt they had been teasing his visit as though it would not happen but might draw *me* out in anticipation. I understood that amongst these groups there were hierarchies and sometimes you never got right to the top but for reasons of control and secrecy, there were always carrots dangled and given that we had put it out there that Thailand seemed to be where you could get away with it, it was actually relatively simple and straightforward that we did find ourselves a few weeks later on the settee with this much revered man. I felt we were heading somewhere.

'It was good to see your picture,' he said.

But this was really an early marker of control. He *had* received it and he was letting us know. British but claiming dual nationality, we were unclear as to whether he was playing his residency for his own end. He chose to live there. Was it simply to profit from a different set of rules.

I realise reading this your thoughts may turn to Gary Glitter. His arrest was in 1997 and mostly for crimes in Cambodia and Vietnam. You may conclude that there was a 'market' there around this time. This was, of course, what we were trying to establish though none of it in relation to the disgraced 1970s icon. His story gives the area and the crimes prominence. Our intelligence confirms that was just the headline act.

And this guy was eccentric, almost like a drag queen. He wanted to be noticed and probably would never have been accepted in the UK. His attire could draw you to conclude that Thailand might be where he made mischief but you could not base a case on that.

His hair was not natural – dyed dark above his expensive flamboyant shirts bought on the cheap in Bangkok. He was almost Glitteresque.

If Stephen pussy-footed around with risqué implication by innuendo, then *his* mannerisms left nothing short for the imagination.

The touchy-feely in the group went up a notch. He would stick his tongue out and declare 'I have a very big tongue'.

He hid from nothing – every remark laced with innuendo.

You could only imagine how he was with close friends.

It was very hard to know if the original group were his best mates at home or indeed he was just someone they looked up to and who had facilitated similar trips though nobody said as much. I could never really understand the link between him and Stephen's group except they clearly knew each other and had met several times.

But they were in awe of him. He was a magnet. With time, he would have been perfect for a sting.

He held himself with a lot of authority, which is staggering really. These people, in their profiles, were always cited for control issues and yet they seemed subservient to a man whom they claimed to really only see a couple of times of year. It left you wondering where the hierarchy began and ended, and even if you appeared top of your local tree, how other branches might climb above you. If you analyse it, control is abuse, and these exerted at least one of those.

'We might want to come – we like a good party,' I offered.

And he needed little encouragement.

He began touching me in the restaurant. I knew that I was being observed by one other member of the group with whom I had less contact. This is how they worked. Watch for the stone-faced one. He is the problem. He is the guy watching and is the danger man.

'What a lovely shirt… how soft,' our Thai friend offered.

He began to run his finger down the middle – Is he looking for the wire?

I held firm. I couldn't flinch, or worse, sweat. I just kept thinking – please don't find it, or more problematical – don't knock it so it comes away.

It just proves that in training you cannot envisage every scenario. We might have code for 'I need to go to the loo to change the tapes' which would inevitably be 'I am not feeling 100 %' but you had to wear a wire somewhere and it sounds obvious retrospectively but nobody had considered that I would get touched up in broad daylight in a restaurant. Yes – you drill a scenario where you might be asked to get naked but you simply extract at that point in the operation.

There had been no suggestion that anything beyond mild touchy-feely was likely amongst them but then one of golden rules was to be wary of outsiders coming into the group. Exactly this. Like the photo. We had to meet the man from Thailand but it was starting from scratch and we couldn't know how he would be and did not expect this. Beware the wild card – even though he was our only way of getting to the next stage.

If he had used two fingers would he have found it? In my head was the recovery position – knock a drink over to change the dynamics. It would draw everyone into the conversation and could take a couple of minutes to clear up. From that, it would be very difficult to re-capture the 'moment'. I didn't want to play that card unless I had to. I had to take him as close as I could to authenticity without throwing in an obstacle that he could reflect on afterwards as doubtful where I might have got away with it at the time. In short, I literally did have to take him down to the wire.

Up and down his hands went on my sleeves.

I don't know if it was obvious to anyone watching but he was un-subtle in such a public place. Like sportsmen who visualise victory and not defeat, I drew strength from the few previous such encounters I had experienced on other jobs. I focussed on the gay bar in Earls Court where I was constantly being touched up from behind. I expected that I would be man-handled at some point on the job but not in the restaurant. I knew that this was when only personal skills could diffuse the situation. There was no physical danger but you could not underestimate the cunning of a child sex offender. My reactions might destroy the job. You were as much in their game as an adult, as the children whose lives they would destroy.

I made my excuses but not to change the tapes this time, and when I came back, he just upped it a notch, rubbing my back and stroking my knees. It was so obvious what was going on yet the rest of the group sat there expressionless as if they had all been assigned rules or knew which ones to assume. The chatty friend was a sideshow – beware the silent assassin observing for information.

This is where training kicks in – that key stage back in the room in London before any of this began, to learn the non-reaction but then to feign the 'I quite like it' response and balancing both. I must knock him back whilst still letting him come on to me. A hissy fit at rejection could blow the lot, yet clearly you couldn't take him further than where he was. Nous and mental strength keep you levelled. It was clear that if I could act the role then nothing was going to happen in the restaurant. Crucially, it was a situation from which I could extract myself without escalating any fear on my part or arousing suspicion on theirs. I had to stay with it and see it through.

He rubbed my back continuously. This was part test and part flamboyance. I am sure they did not think we were police. Their guard would have been up more so for journalists. And had he come within a whisker of finding my wire as his hands once again obsessed over my soft shirt.

'Are you flirting with me?' I said, knowing that speech gave my body a chance to move, re-arrange position and release the transfixed spell he was trying to cast over me but seemed to be caught up in too.

Flicking his medium-length blonde air and his blue eyes never releasing their glare, he just smiled.

It was classic predator. It said test, control and abuse.

He told me that he had a boy back in Thailand who did everything for him. He left the insinuation there. I understood what he meant.

'Why don't you live there full time?' I asked, knowing deep down that there was something in this.

'I still want my roots here.'

He seemed to have no reason to be in the UK. It felt that his needs were fulfilled in Asia. He knew he could fall well under the radar there. Many Brits were also heading there.

I tried to break him off by re-engaging with the circle but in group dynamics there is always a leader who commands attention and focus and he held that rank.

'Are you enjoying this?' he asked a couple of times.

I had to stay in a zone, focussed so George knew to interact. He could deflect some curve balls I might not want to deal with.

'Did you like the photo?' my friend asked.

'Yeah, yeah, yeah,' he answered dismissively so as not to be side-tracked by the interruption.

I didn't flinch once but his strange, sadistic manner did give me goose bumps. All the time I had known the group there was never any suggestion amongst them that this kind of exhibitionism was their modus operandi. He stood out in his behaviour and his standing. They looked up to him. I can't reason as to what happened that enabled them to take my relationship of 'friendship' with an undercurrent that was never spoken of beyond 'parties' to this point where I had unlocked another level.

Still the group behaved as they always had around me. They had their secrets, for sure. Intel suggested so. But they had done their job now in introducing me to the man from Thailand. What would happen next? Was I being lined up as some conduit between him, sex tourism and the UK – some sort of patsy that they had found, adopted, examined and felt they had confidently but silently indoctrinated to be the front man for their needs and desires overseas? Were they trying to push me forward to make their mistakes and leave me high and dry? Had they all had a similar public groping as part of their own scrutiny with him?

As their most recent inductee, I know I was being tested for something beyond Wales, yet they as a group had given me little hard evidence that I could walk away with. I knew one thing which gave me the confidence that we had done well. He had clearly spoken to the group and despite the suspicion when I went to see the man with the military background, my vetting had been allowed to proceed this far.

In other words, our operation was almost textbook. Our surveillance, our techniques, our points of entry, our patience and our reactions had passed every test in a game where you could not know what the questions were.

We had arrived at the point where many of the group anticipated our visits and that they were looking forward to seeing us again. When really put under the microscope, even George who so nearly had been proven right by thinking it was not worth the risk wearing a wire, had to ask me where it was hidden. I duped him too.

I hadn't told him before. He didn't need that knowledge. It was just a small piece of information that might stop his eyes from fixating on it and he may well have done. But he hadn't seemed to find it and we somehow survived that scrutiny.

One month later, I returned alone to Wales. I had to see if there had been an adverse reaction after his return to Thailand and I was told by our unit to tidy up the loose ends.

There hadn't been a problem but we were pulling out.

It was important that we didn't just disappear. We couldn't know if we would infiltrate another ring with whom this group's paths might cross. It was vital to tidy it up so I made one last trip, feigned a few tears and told them George was more ill than I thought and we had to forget the whole property dream.

I knew we had done well. Up to a point. When the job ended, I realised how draining it was. Months of work had gone into this and we were probably just a couple of steps away from casting the net further.

Except of course, it was highly unlikely that ops would extend the job to Thailand because of cost, legislation and extradition treaties, plus at this time the practicalities of surveillance out there.

That is why I could happily throw out there the readiness to party but I also had to shun it with Stephen. It was a difficult balancing act knowing that a group gathering could take you to the heart of the story but the tale could write itself without your control. There was no danger with Mr Thailand. It didn't ever look like we were going to go out there.

On reflection, that questions the ethos of mission one. But, the carrot of Bangkok could have exposed what was going on in the UK proving that the seeds for sex tourism did not begin because you jumped on the plane. They started at home. Plus, as the Glitter story shows, the hunch was right even though the legislation in 1994 was not ready to go.

The legislation and the infancy of the project had hit its first brick wall.

12

I was now back in the North dealing with my speciality in stolen property. I felt realistic enough to understand what we had learned and achieved in Wales but flat too in that we had not been allowed to progress.

It had been a decent outing. My training was certainly enhanced. I learnt a lot about me. I was 100% certain that this was a job I had to do even though in the beginning it was all gut feeling from George that it was right for me and there was little expertise in the field to show you the way.

I was now more determined than ever. Wales had given me a glimpse.

My space had been invaded but I had survived it. In total I was alone nine times with Stephen to the point that I stopped taking brochures as we were now 'friends'.

I understood too from George, my superiors and the psychologist Tom that 'failure' was as likely as success in this kind of work and that beyond the mental contamination that this field could play on your home life, the individual had to be realistic about what could be achieved – especially against the still limited legislation.

I was keen to crack on but it was not as though these jobs were rolling off the conveyor belt. I am sure that with the knowledge of today people will appreciate that this is 1994 and intelligence gathering was painstaking, the Internet was almost in its infancy, resources and our own knowledge were slim and that the police were wary and proceeding with caution.

However, there was commitment. That manifested itself in a trip. It was decided we *should* go abroad for three days.

There was no job. We weren't tracking anybody. As the old joke goes, it was all research, sir. Except it was. Much of the operational data and previous submissions from victims and predators unsurprisingly kept revolving around two places. Thailand was clearly on the radar and the next was Holland.

All roads led to Amsterdam.

We would spend around 72 hours entering ridiculously hardcore, pitch-black venues like The Cock Ring with flashing lights to direct you towards the area with chains. We would watch, absorb and store knowledge.

Why were we doing this? It was like feeding the sub-conscience. We were investing in future scenarios. We were trying to think like they do. We understood that conversations ahead might mean common ground could be around those great trips to the free culture of The Netherlands.

It is hard to explain to a friend over a beer. This was George's idea and we had to justify it to work, of course, but it was not a hard sell. Eight of us went in all. It was taken that seriously. If you put it on a tax return or indeed in my own expenses to the force to an unknowing accountant, it would be probably greeted with derision but I can tell you now with hindsight that it was one of the most significant decisions that we made as a family unit.

We flew out early on various morning flights from around the country. Airports attract all sorts of people with different agendas. In amongst the lads in their late teens on that flight to Schipol, many people were looking for the same. And so were we. The difference was that we were not there to enjoy. Our mission was to learn.

That, as a brief, once again returns to the conditioned environment. Here was a place that sprung to life well into the afternoon, fuelled by alcohol and legalised drugs with prostitution perhaps more available and certainly more advertised than any other developed city in Europe. It had carnage written all over it.

Against that backdrop, beauty and bikes…daffodils and dykes. The canal culture and the happy-go-lucky cyclist met history halfway. Many people on their raucous weekends would sober up with a dose of the past – the Anne Frank Museum in the house where she hid with her family from Nazi Germany whilst writing her diaries from a hidden annexe remain a poignant leveller in a city of excess.

We had to walk that line too. There was no point in us being defined by our job on this trip. Research meant more than remembering bars and quirky features of the sex industry. We had to do normal things that people experienced before they got reckless or pursued their vices and that meant simple things like understanding our credibility would be poor if we didn't have a working memory of places like the main railway station, through which most tourists would pass at some point.

The normal life had to be in the recall as much as the outrageous, which ultimately many might not remember at all.

We checked into a medium sized hotel – basic and pleasant, not too flash but typically normal just down from the main square, and then set to work.

We would build rapport with bar staff to make it real. Conversations amongst ourselves would not live long in the memory but individuals working the scene would form character portraits from which we could pull stereotypes or genuine anecdotes if we needed to show that credibility in the future.

We would often take a card from a venue too so that in time we could place it in a wallet which might become a prop. It also served as a steer if we needed to *invent* memories. We went anywhere we could to acquire knowledge and would break regularly to discuss traits and characteristics, many of which were repeated over and over again. You don't know what you are looking for or what you might need, you just had to absorb and part of that process meant photography. Nothing said you were there more than actual pictures and some of those might walk or cross a line. In time as the technology advanced, the likelihood of storing these on a phone would become apparent and then the images became part of the game of what to share with 'new friends' and when to show it but at least you could justify what you were saying. The experience in Wales had left that one scar – namely that a photo of me was out there somewhere. In a totally different context, I knew that the mouth could move and tell lies but as the old saying goes, the camera never does. Imagery from this trip could serve me well in the years ahead.

I took a boat trip – because people did. I took coffee at the main station and bought rubbish from a shop so the memory of the steps up to it and the smell of the bread, granules of coffee and the noise of the announcements would never leave me. I knew first hand after the job in Wales that paedophiles did not just talk about paedophilia if in fact at all. They talked around it and that meant any chat about Amsterdam would be in the mundane rather than the specific so these details were paramount in learning my Dutch identity.

We did obvious things like an Ajax stadium tour or eating in a greasy fry up or an Argentinian Steak House. Equally we could say that we didn't have time for other sites like the Heineken Museum but that didn't mean it wouldn't be a conversation starter. You could add to your credibility if you said 'we did most of the tourist bits but missed out on...' and your natural conversation might then involve someone who did. You were trying to establish normality whilst knowing that there was a common perhaps unspoken ground that in most trips to Amsterdam there was a something else going on.

To be able to reel off multiple experiences, locations or individual names of premises would make us sound credible.

The trip also could narrow the conversation faster. Real life experience tells you that if somebody mentions a trip to the Dutch capital, it is almost inevitable that soon the talk turns to the cafes (and the drugs) or the sights you see in the window. It was becoming clear, without ever knowing when you might need to pull this trip out of the memory bank that it cut out so many obstacles in the cat and mouse game of being entrusted by the type of person we wished to infiltrate, and there was no better example of that then what we had experienced in Wales when similar talk of Thailand raised the stakes. The difference was that we hadn't done the knowledge and been there nor were we likely to head out to Asia specifically in the field at this point.

Lesson learned though. Indeed, the majority of our time was spent doing the mundane – about 10 % of the trip was at the seedy end of the deal.

One such place in time would pay dividends. We stumbled soberly across a pole-dancing venue in a three-storey building. That detail is key.

Up the stairs we went to the first floor. There was often that air of mystery in your bones that climbing from the street to a higher level installed in you in Amsterdam. Anticipation perhaps or a sense of the unknown that made only the neon signs visible from the street. A long corridor followed. I am sure this was all part of the experience. Anticipation, yes.

This was *The Blue Boy and Why Not*. We knew what was coming but yet you feel like you are walking into danger. We had to get into the role. Ordinarily, none of us would frequent places like this unless for research but whilst many such places shared the same characteristics, they were all different too – or felt so – if you were not used to this kind of scene.

We emerged into a small bar area with a few seats around.

If you turned to your left, there was a video screen. Everything was showing homosexual acts. It was clear what we had walked into. Then there were another three TVs and, to your left and right, cameras. There was also a further set of stairs which obviously presented mystery but was clearly where stuff happened.

We would always make for the bar. Talking to the staff casually would be where you would learn the most. You would gain nothing from chatting to each other. Plus, if you happened to go there more than once and they remembered you then your anecdotal recall was stronger and so was theirs if it ever came to that.

Across the bar were menus. It was here you could order. Not cocktails or burgers but whatever your sexual appetite was required could be served on a plate. I had never seen anything so forward. It was a new level in knowledge and further re-skilling in that non-reactionary face which then had to respond positively. And it was all there – photos and images of young-looking males and once you had decided, you would place your order at the counter and wait to be directed to the stairs and a floor of individual cubicles separated only by doors.

I had never seen it so organised – all against this backdrop of loud music and explicit videos. Its clientele were multi-national which confirmed what we already knew. This problem was not exclusive to respected old men in raincoats back in the UK. It was worldwide.

It showed the importance of not going alone. The footage of three or four guys on one another may have been on the screen but it was the kind of place where you could find yourself rounded upon and intimidated if in the minority.

In front of the bar staff, all of whom without exception were homosexual, I flicked the book sometimes at haste or perhaps slower pretending to browse, then would put it down only to feign further interest. They offered the book to others and asked me if I fancied anything on the menu. I flat-batted them with my standard 'nothing catches my eye just yet'. It was possibly the most sexually alienating experience of my life. Wherever you looked it was in your face – a far cry from Old Compton Road and few people getting touchy-feely in the gents. This was constant. Almost with aggression. There was no let-off.

It became the pattern – a bar or two and something normal, then a de-brief, making notes on everything. Prices could vary of course, but also catch you out. Obviously, it was important to know ballpark figures for paying for sexual activity, pints of beer or slices of cake along with boat trips and train fares. Location was king; its context might save your life in the future. Wales had already taught about passing credibility tests. You had to know Amsterdam.

We identified six or seven key spots for recall. Our story would always be as bland as 'we went there to enjoy ourselves'. To that end, I needed to have that background awareness of the 'scene' but be normal enough to rave about their cheeses or the cured bacon at 'that lovely little place we went for breakfast with all the football shirts on the wall'.

In the same way that it took so long for Wales to put anything on the table and it would always be that cat and mouse game, we too had to adopt that approach. In essence when you try to infiltrate, you are selling yourself to a new circle. That means you adopt the same cagey stance as those people. You don't go in there and say you have been to The Cock Ring in Amsterdam, you build up your trip story with bland normality letting the stench of your motives whiff silently as the undercurrent. Learning how to manage the speed with which you released information was as important as knowing how to break someone. You talk about Ajax and the canals first.

You had to have been there.

Today, you could cut and paste information into your own brain and possibly get away with it and that would be fine to a point except it removes all sensation from the experience so you would never ever be able to befriend a 'fellow' paedophile with your 'feelings' about the place. You could list bars and prices like a robot but you would get caught out and run out of vocabulary if you hadn't been there for real.

You had to be there.

For George, that meant checking out canal boats. In the work ahead, we knew that we would be dealing again with people with specific hobbies so we should have one too. George was into barges and they were obviously unavoidable in Amsterdam.

There was a reasonable chance that this hobby could be shared with somebody ahead and even for the less enthusiastic, taking to water in Holland was a probable over a possible so it was a sensible punt. Tourists did boat trips, full stop.

We absorbed everything we could – except a weekend. Heaven only knows if it got crazier on a Saturday and Sunday bit we saw enough to know people were regularly queuing and that business was thriving.

Instinctively, I had good recall. Naturally, and through training. So many of the bars' names stayed with me and even if in time I might find myself saying to a target 'what is the name of that place called The Cock something?' I could still enhance my credibility by remembering the street if was off or the bike hire opposite. People did often talk like that some time after a holiday and it is the easiest way to engage in conversation by offering solid facts but then by feigning a gap in your knowledge.

Amsterdam was the easiest place in my career to go undercover in broad daylight. It taught me well and encouraged me once again. This work *was* vital and even though Wales now seemed like a training exercise and we had achieved nothing yet, my mind was re-focussed. I didn't mind running my informants and operational commitments in the Regional

Crime Squad but this was my priority.

I was waiting for a job.

When we returned home, we knew the knowledge was important and were pushing for trips to Germany, Poland and Romania in particular and of course, Thailand and other countries in Asia where we were now aware that children were sold for sex for as little as £1.

I was adamant that we should also *return* to Amsterdam, not put off by whispers from those outside the group back at work that it had all been a jolly. Management were supportive and understood the role. Yes, it was great to be able to work on your own steam, stay in a hotel and fly abroad but you could not put in a time sheet or place a financial value on acquiring intelligence. Every officer spent their career doing just that in some capacity. The difference is that this was specialist and unchartered territory.

Blind eyes were turned everywhere across the planet to what was going on. Except now we could see them.

13

The fact remained that until the work came to us, I had to wait, remaining in my 'normal' job as an undercover operative.

In 1995, I had a breakthrough.

We were two years down the line on and off with this project with no obvious signs of success except the ability to pat ourselves on the back that we were approaching it correctly.

During the lull, I felt flat. I needed something. Just a little spark to remind everyone and myself the value of this work. And for all that we planned, trained, researched and second-guessed, my first arrest in this field was relatively straightforward and followed almost none of the drills we had conditioned ourselves to, which in itself was a lesson in the reminder that there are no rules and every job invents new ones.

I got a call saying that an individual in the Home Counties wanted someone to supply a child. Much of the intel in scenarios like this came from prostitutes (or street workers as they are known today) who fed us loose talk – themselves naively entrusted by clients who felt safe talking to those already engaging in illegalities.

But we had worked those patches and by and large left them to their own devices. Some were generous with information and in return and that led us to this sting. In the 1980s we had generally viewed them as criminals. Something changed in the 1990s which placed them as good sources.

As an officer, I valued the information I would get from prostitutes. Some had the reputation of being unreliable and dangerous, possibly due to their habits or vulnerability but nobody should have any doubt that some had morals and they knew too that somebody wanting a child was a line crossed.

I simply had to play a role.

My phone rang and we spoke. He told me what he wanted, for how long and I gave him the cost around the £200 figure. And the meet was set. I didn't really take time to reflect that I was placing a sum of money against an innocent child beyond the credibility that I knew this was sadly near the going rate.

This time, there was no working an individual or a group over a period of time. It was a straight transaction. There was of course this kind of work. It was an instant hit and needed to be done because ultimately it saved a child but the bigger picture was far greater. This was an individual fulfilling his dirty needs for an afternoon, not part of some bigger net where you could attempt to shut down a ring en masse.

It was still vital – remember, it is all about the child. Save one child.

So I agreed to meet him at a low budget hotel and went to the room first to recce in good time. I left two plain-clothed officers in there waiting for him.

The 'client' and I agreed our rendezvous as the lobby and since the legislation once again limited our powers of arrest, and because I was mindful of not being seen to entrap (even though he had instigated all of this) I asked him again for the benefit of my wire and the tapes that would air in court 'are you sure you really want to do this?'

Of course, standard operational procedure now meant that I went over what we had talked about on the phone for the benefit of the recording solely to prove that he had placed that call.

It just made him more frenzied working himself into a state of fever pitch excitement.

He handed me the money and I gave him the room key and sent him on his way. For my part, the work was done. I was more a facilitator acting than performing slow painstaking undercover work.

From my voice on the phone, I had obviously appeared confident and trustworthy. By the time we came face to face, his eye was so far off the ball with anticipation that I barely had to work hard at all, except to preserve the evidence.

I went up in the lift with him and parted, watching him walk into his own demise, turning through the labyrinth of this cheap hotel which befitted the occasion, only to turn the key slowly into the assigned room and be met by my colleagues. My eyes marked him all the way to the door.

He had been a fool and betrayed many of the methods I would come up against over the years. His security was lapse and for his naivety and vile personal fulfilment he received 18 months. The job was done. There was no child at risk. There was no child. Not, this time.

As it stood at the time, the only way we could legitimately take him down was to file a charge of him inciting me to supply a person with a child for sex.

The greater concern was twofold. It seems unlikely that it would have been a first offence and equally, the systems to avoid re-offending were not in place. It was highly likely that there was insufficient deterrent and he could be back here again or possibly fall under the radar with his guard much higher next time having learnt his lesson only in terms of his personal security rather than the wrongdoing of his action.

Today, at the time of writing, it is estimated that there are 600 to 900 offenders per police force in England and Wales. They may well have been there when we started this journey. We couldn't know. Except that it had to begin. So when you read horrific contemporary cases now in the digital era, the drive for justice began around 1994 with moments like this but even two years in, I had been uncertain if I was continuing with the work.

Just a little 'victory' like this renewed my faith and those around me. Sometimes winning the internal argument became just as important as the work, but every small success was vindication.

This particular job came with no pressure. Later that day I went back to the station and carried on with my admin. It was that simple.

Yet, it was a breath of fresh air and I needed to continue believing. Amsterdam was excellent work and I couldn't know where it would sit in future operations and that in itself was slightly stressful having to carry that knowledge around waiting for the day. Wales was also tense because progress was slow and there was the unknown of the photo, just who this guy from Thailand was, and our inability to get to that bigger picture.

This was a breeze and personified the ups and downs of police work and specialist activity. An arrest that we hadn't worked hard over nailed a conviction. But others whom we tracked for months evaded us.

Something had to give. Patience would always be required but I felt that success lay somewhere in the middle. Little did I know that the disciplines of Wales *would* meet the pay-off from the Home Counties.

I was just a few months away from an operation that would change policing and the legislation forever.

14

'We missed you,' said one of my superiors. 'For five years.'

1996 I returned officially to Cleveland Police after an attachment that long to the Regional Crime Squad. But I was always here and there and 'away'.

My normal undercover work had taken me around the country, doing infiltrations flushing out stolen property, works of art and drugs. My secondment to the Regional Crime Squad had led me to renew old friendships within the Met and, on the other side of the fence. Commendations had come and gone and such work with my informants had led to multiple arrests and convictions.

Specialised units like the 'Flying Squad' were arresting crooks in the act of committing robberies, which was an incredible feeling when it takes over your secondment and brings it to a conclusion after witnessing the painstaking methods serious criminals would use. It was equally satisfying as it was potentially the unit that I could have been associated with in my Met days. To get a taste of it was brilliant.

So-called 'friends' had trusted me. They knew I would not place them at risk and whatever money they were paid they got despite the stories in my Met days that for some sources grasses did not get the money. To the best of my knowledge we always paid.

Once again, I had to deal with the same old same old politics with some officers getting jealous, suggesting that my friends were better used by officers within the Met rather than someone working long distance. That is their opinion but it did not overly matter as running informants eventually came to an end – not before one last detail of the job. You could still never be sure if you would run into these people again. Criminals were criminals after all and most of them had been very useful and so it was only fair that I saw them all personally in a way that was far more personal than the cold phone call often wrapping up relations with a couple of beers before we parted company!

Do you get attached? A little. It is not easy running people with hectic lives who tell lies and they are criminals who will carry on doing their job. Informants take massive risks too.

One such friend was very poorly and in hospital after major surgery. He was a real tough old guy but in a bad state. I still felt it important to arrange a trip down to see him.

'You travelled all this way to see me? He asked.

'What are friends for?' I replied.

The truth is that we had a very good relationship and he did leave a void. Sometimes you had to walk away but I felt that you always had to end these relationships as though they were genuine. You didn't just disappear. You tidied it up.

We had reached a slight crossroads. Cleveland wanted me back. That was fine of course but I sensed other work would come calling.

Returning to your force can be unsettling especially when some managers were content on suggesting that my undercover days were now behind me and others were far more accommodating. Like anything, if you make sacrifices and work hard specialist skills means you do not really want to give it up.

Still, I was waiting for the next job that I felt now was the kind of work to focus on exclusively. I continued to read up and tried to acquire knowledge as to the speed with which other countries were reacting to the paedophile problem.

It emerged that legislation around the world was pretty ancient too and this took time to change but one significant piece of news came in from the States. You probably recall Megan's Law.

This was the first big breakthrough at a time when American and Britain were considered to be ahead of the field but still way behind the ballgame of what the reality was. Megan Kanka had been raped and brutally murdered at just seven years old by her neighbour in Mercer County, New Jersey in 1994.

Jesse K. Timmendequas lured her next door, sexually assaulted her and then strangled her. Significantly he had two previous convictions for similar against young girls.

One month after her death, the legislation changed meaning that all sex offenders had to now register where before it had been only partially enacted. Crucially too, the public had a right to know if such an individual was within their midst. Websites, newspapers and pamphlets could all display such information. It had taken a horror act to get to this far. Britain was not yet there but would have its own Megan moment in the decade that followed. America had made a start towards disclosure even if prevention was no easier to effect.

The UK was watching America and working with them. George and I were at the start of a very long process in the smallest of specialised units facing the most mammoth of tasks and a job that would never ever be complete.

I was desperate to get back into this world, Still though, the work in Wales and Amsterdam had not paid dividends. I knew too that we had probably missed many opportunities to progress given the archaic laws of the day. I had to be patient. The force had supported me in allowing my secondment to work they knew little about. I wanted to give it back.

One operation would have a defining moment in my undercover career. In the years that followed I have used certain extracts during presentations but to this day the majority remains locked away in my mind.

Until now.

15

'Are you available to do a particular job?'

It was October 1997 and I knew exactly what this meant.

'Yes, I would like to,' I replied without knowing much more.

I did not want my experience to turn cold. I had been waiting far too long. This is undoubtedly the work that I trained for. There was also little preparation for what lay ahead.

The support team had done much of the pre-work before that call came in. I was somewhere down the food chain. I knew, of course, that the *system* had been up and running for some months before they assigned me. I was just joining the story. It was a speculative punt in the dark. The intel had been gathered and it was time to swoop.

My Assistant Chief Constable was made aware and I began that process of regularly going missing again. After years of nothing, I had to get back into that mindset – that very mentality I had been training for I now had to re-find, and I knew the pressure was on.

Nobody put it in those terms but clearly it was going to accelerate the work for myself if we ran a successful operation to its conclusion this time. Amsterdam would be deemed essential not a luxury and secondments would be imperative not arousing suspicion.

That lay in the background. The pressure of the job was essentially the job and once again that all started with that one opportunity to make a first impression.

And I knew little except that the individual ticked all the boxes. He was considered high risk and likely to abuse boys in parks or train stations. Beyond that not much more other than that my superiors considered him unlikely to knock me back.

He had recently been released from prison after less than a year inside for what really should have been a five-year stretch. As part of his release conditions he had to stay at a halfway house as was often the way with sex offenders and some criminals. We, at least, had that in place in 1997. But, he came with many alarm bells.

The halfway house meant that the police and the probation services were keeping an eye on him. He had check in and exit times that had to be strongly adhered to. If he breached them, the authorities had to be clear he had done so and it was not a mistake on their part.

He was allowed nowhere where people would congregate nor was he allowed to travel at times children might be expected to. He had to be back at the halfway house by then. We knew he had associations and connections. Who they were was the end game.

I was excited but I did not want to overload myself with information. I trusted my instinct and our techniques. I reminded myself that the work we had done so far had gone pretty much to plan, and it was somebody else's decision when a mission ended. I sensed too that the appetite was now back where it was at the beginning and whilst we could not take on multiple jobs at the same time, there was an increasing understanding that there was plenty of work out there in this field.

It was time to meet. Or at least, attempt to.

We had done numerous dummy runs, isolating in our minds the route he would take and the likely scenario where we would engage for the first time. I played it over in mind, preparing by visualising that encounter and then stepping back to relax so I appeared natural. This was the problem with intelligence and why you never wanted more than you needed. All that mattered to me was my cover story, my opening line and being able to identify him.

He was very well built – strapping, seemed pleasant from afar and not threatening. He probably viewed himself the same, given that these people could not have the error of their ways explained to them. He undoubtedly could handle himself.

This was Edwin from the North of England.

Because of his virtual house arrest, the 'intercept' had to be 10 am. I had only one agenda: attempt to engage, hold his attention and arrange to meet again – all within a narrow time frame.

That window was 20 minutes and on a bus. That was it. The maximum. And we hadn't even started yet. My adrenaline was pumping. I needed to get all but alongside him. He was very much set in his ways. He would always be on the bus.

But it had to be the right bus: the bus that you know that nine times out of ten he will remain on for that maximum time limit. This is pressure.

I was on a high waiting for him, wondering if this was going to happen. Operational support gave me the reassurance that he was on his way. I needed to mix that pumped up focus with patience and normality. I mustn't push it.

I had watched him for several weeks walking to the bus stop. His behaviour was clockwork – mostly because of his release hours. But I couldn't control which bus he would get on nor the order in which other people would board it. We needed to head into the city centre and I clearly had no control of where he might go and I certainly could not get on before him.

I had to be prepared to be frustrated. If it wasn't right today, it would have to wait.

I am watching him now like never before. The bus comes round the corner and it's time. We are dealing in seconds and he has no idea that I am just a couple of passengers behind him in the queue. He knows in the halfway house he is being observed and that as long as he returns on time and behaves himself that suspicion will ease but this is his freedom when he thinks the police have better things to do. He can mingle in and make his next move, He can wander freely in amongst his prey. He can hide in broad daylight undertaking the mundane like boarding a bus.

But so can I.

I climb on hesitantly – eyes running at double vision half watching him but making sure I am not watching him at all. He makes for the back of the bus and I head the same way, pulling up in the seat the row forward from him.

This is my moment to engage. It is now or never. What is, after all, the right moment to start talking? He may only be on the bus for three stops.

I ask a question I could not ask if I had been on the bus any length of time.

'Is this for the town centre?' I blandly enquire.

Was that even the right question? It was a bog standard for anybody on public transport, so perhaps so.

'I need to get to the train station,' I followed up.

I had already ticked two boxes. I made him that expert by seeking his knowledge and I knew that he loved buses and trains. The file had earmarked the latter as a potential place for picking up young boys and no time in prison would really quench that thirst.

He also had a habit of visiting gay saunas just to fulfil his needs but always then cutting it fine with his curfew. For now, I would leave that

74

option behind and stick with the stereotypical trainspotter mentality.

It had to be the right question. I could not after all be back at the bus stop at the same time next week and begin the process again. There was no second chance. I could only ask the same person once if this was the bus for the town centre or the train station. He had to bite now or the mission was toast before it began.

The pre-team had established all of this. It was up to my pride and communication skills not to let anyone down. This is how you feel. It was time to use that knowledge without feeling a desperation to nail it. I am confident, as I was in Wales but he could have just got up and walked away at any time. It is quite likely that he rarely spoke to anyone outside of his circle. His contact with normality was minimal so I have to back myself that he would engage with me.

The bus is busy but not packed.

'It's my first time in the area,' I expand – my Southern accent possibly making him safe and me more credible.

And I was in.

He had taken the bait. We were up and running and in three simple sentences, he had let his guard down or shown his naivety. At any point he could have disengaged but this was enough. From here, I knew I could work him and veer towards a second meet.

I implied that I did not live too far away – the implication therefore that I would be back.

'I never had an interest in coming to the City,' I told him as if marvelling that now I had found a friend I couldn't believe my luck that it had all worked out perfectly. He was a loner. So was I. It was a place for him to start in the new outside world.

'Are you wanting to go to the railway station?' he re-iterated.

We were instantly comfortable with each other.

I can't explain why he was drawn to me. He must have trusted few but also against the confinement of prison and the halfway house, perhaps it was easy to engage with *anyone* who appeared normal or mundane. Maybe it was a relief to him. I couldn't at that stage have looked obviously like a man who might share a gay sauna with him.

And then we are exchanging numbers. We hooked up very naturally.

I agree to call him in a couple of days.

'Can I just double-check your number?' I run a standard drill.

To ask once would be a schoolboy error. And his guard was down.

Looking back, it sounds and reads so simple but it was only because of the knowledge acquired, the planning instigated and the skills honed.

This was routine police work but still very easy to get wrong. He came just short of the railway station. We parted there. There was no reason to complicate my story by him following me to the platform. I made for the information kiosk as if to buy a ticket. I got a coffee and sat it out. I waited a while then called it in. I didn't need to feign taking a journey. I had total faith in those supporting me. I couldn't just wander back into town. We had a car tailing the bus and another following him as we said goodbye. In a few moments, they would be picking me up.

I had walked down the streets elated. The worst was over and the initial contact could not have gone better, but the next time would be just as hard for different reasons. It had been so easy and a perfect drill. We had identified the opportunity, made the contact and exited at the ideal moment with the subsequent meet arranged. Knowing when to approach and in the right manner at the right time in the right place was some luck but also a large element of skill and this was textbook. It was also a test of communication skills.

I felt very comfortable with him. He was a big lad who could turn nasty. Nobody had any clue where this would lead except that he had loomed large on the radar as a risk.

I had studied everything about him and he nothing of me, but of course, I had to park that knowledge to get to know him 'properly' and differentiate between what the file said and what he had told me. I could not introduce something that I knew but in the context of us, didn't. I had to ignore the dossier now.

Operational heads were ecstatic that in such a narrow window we had made contact. Job done. For now. We were under way.

16

When I called a couple of days later, I had to remind him who I was. I also knew his 'parole' hours so obviously proposed something right at the first possible window of opportunity. There was no point in meeting him if he had to be back within 90 minutes or so.

'I've a dear friend and I have promised to show him the area,' I placed my 'legend' on the table. 'I am just looking for a few places to visit. I owe that to him.'

Whether or not he would ultimately materialise, that friend would be George once more or someone within our small band and of course, I was playing a similar card to Wales. You wouldn't see George much because he didn't get out much. Mobility was not his strength. They were my lines.

We talked for twenty minutes and it just flew by.

'I am from round here so I might be able to help,' he offered.

I was watching every word I said for the future when I might need to recall it.

I felt though his guard was coming down.

It was impossible to know if he thought I was his type (for him), his type (in that we were looking for the same) or he just thought he had made a friend in a world where he would always struggle to do so. It could have been any of the three but I was mindful too of the case studies which showed that these individuals often looked for a meal ticket. Most had little money or a car. To be seen to be that was often the easiest way to bonding in the months of silent gamesmanship before anybody puts anything significant on the table.

'I had some bad experiences of getting on the wrong buses,' I had lied on the bus in our first meeting, allowing dips in the conversation so it had seemed natural.

Pauses were good for both parties – time to reflect, nor the need to force it. But I had left him with that message that I was not from here and had come for a purpose. On that, the trust was built.

But on our second visit he upped the ante immediately. He had met me at the railway station, shook my hand and asked if I fancied a drink straight away. I knew exactly where he was taking me.

'Do you know what this is?' he asked.

I ordered and orange juice to his half a lager. I couldn't really get into the part beyond that. I could not betray the tape.

'Yeah, it's an OK bar,' I replied.

He put his hand on my knee.

'This is a gay bar,' he invited a response.

He had a clear agenda. Now those three options about his motives narrowed themselves down. It didn't mean the other two would not apply. It just meant for now that I was his priority. There were few other people around.

'I've no problem with that,' I flat-batted back.

His hand was still on my knee.

Flashback to Soho and the training with George. I was unlikely to flinch but clearly, I was beyond his meal ticket. I was the main course.

His hand moved to my hand.

I needed to withdraw gracefully. Unleashed from his halfway house and his prison sentence, maybe the frustrations took over. The positive I can take from it is that I was trusted – and early in the relationship.

'Am I the wrong type?' he asked.

My next comment was vital.

'No, you're not the wrong sex.'

I had to keep him hooked without knocking back. I had realised in Wales that this was the default position – to keep them interested in a disinterested position.

'You're just not my type,' I cooled him down.

Nobody could have got this far in twenty minutes – and that applied to both of us.

But he still wanted to meet again. I rejected him but befriended him too. Keep the door open.

I left it a week. To make him want. And he tried it on again the next time. I rebuffed once more whilst trying to get him to think as to why. Then, following time I was there, he didn't mention what had happened in the bar. I was relieved that this was not a hurdle we could not overcome.

He was staying with me without pursuing me.

The game of cat and mouse had begun as I gave him nuggets to analyse. I wanted only one thing – for him to think that we might be like-minded. Leaving him to his thoughts was possibly the most powerful thing I could do.

Equally, I could not push it. When it came to court, it had to have come from him. He had to take the carrots and the innuendo and develop it. Every time we met, the rapport increased. Yet, it was slow and often subtle. He would pass young kids in the street but he wouldn't drop his guard. I would be lucky in the first few weeks if I even caught a glance from him towards minors. There was little to pick up on, not much to report back on – except that we had trust. I introduced two key elements well in advance of not knowing how this would play out.

One of our small unit came with me early in proceedings to authenticate my reason for being there. He was now that mate for whom I was researching my visits in the George role. Also. It was time to plant the seed that my mother was poorly and that from time to time I might need to call her carer if I was likely to be late back.

I would have to wait until something gave.

In the short term that meant walking the beaches of the East Coast. We would go for miles at the height of winter just so I could corroborate my story, talking about everything and nothing and then taking bus after bus, visiting churches, shopping malls and retail centres on a regular basis. And in the long term, that meant fish and chips three months later.

In the interim, we had walked many times around a retail park and shopping arcades – always a magnet for the paedophile. He told me that he had been to Amsterdam. Many had but I doubt for the same reasons as him. My knowledge served me well. Bingo. Common ground. But it was there at the retail park, notionally shopping that he broke it to me and delivered his first real power manoeuvre.

He had told his parole officer that he had met someone and we were in a relationship.

I knew that was *me* – and that was not me, of course.

But I was well aware what he was doing and it was a very good sign. He too was sowing seeds. He had begun the process of incomplete truths. He *had* met me but we were not an item. He was putting the marker down towards stability and that perhaps I might go into the halfway house and we might go out for the day. He was building *his* cover story. And that now meant one thing. He was getting on a train to meet the network.

I was surprised and delighted.

His half-truths were good though. It is uncanny how, on both sides of the police divide, we operated in similar fashion. His modus operandi was so similar to mine. He kept as close to the truth as I did except the big picture remained incomplete. Lies were not dishonesty – they just lacked the whole story so he in fact did open up to confess that he *had* come out of prison.

I knew this, of course, so he did not need to share this but as a measure of trust and an indicator of how close we were, it was colossal. He *was* telling me the truth which was a hell of a lot better than him sending us off on a wild goose chase into a fantasy world of loose ends and second-guessing. It was exactly what we wanted. He followed the script.

Obviously, he was shy on the detail of his imprisonment. I never asked him why he had been inside but he offered the excuse that it was a misunderstanding. This was language I would hear again.

I told him it was not a problem if he wanted me to go to his residence but he never asked outright.

'You can trust me,' I told him.

'I know I can,' he replied and it spoke volumes for our operation.

It was also textbook for him too.

The only doubt I could have was if he was grooming me or using me – but at this point it didn't matter because he *trusted* me enough to consider either. And adults did get groomed too.

It soon emerged it was the latter when I met him for the afternoon for our routine sightseeing and he played his next card.

'You're going off sightseeing but I'm not coming with you,' he announced.

And that's when he *trusted* me to cover for him as he boarded a train towards The Midlands. The network was expecting him.

That was massive. He had used me to break free. The picture *was* bigger.

Little did he know that we then placed surveillance officers on the train and tracked him all the way to his destination. He had no relatives in that area nor any obvious reason to be there. The net was expanding. They had all been waiting for the right time to meet up.

He knew that he had only a limited window within his parole hours and had to be back in time. *We* knew that we were now involving several other forces but within which, there was no counterpart of myself. This was once again new territory.

I needed to find an introduction to whomever he was meeting and at the back of my mind was the perfect plan.

On the next time we would meet I would tell him I was thinking of buying a computer.

17

I delivered it as a throwaway comment. 'I am thinking of buying a computer.' But I knew that this was how his network was operating. When we met after his train excursion, I tried not over-ask about it.

'Oh yeah, it was fine,' he answered as though he had just been to the shops.

I was sowing the seed of doubt in reminding him that I had covered for him without interrogating him as to why. He would note that I had asked and I would register that he had replied little. It would come again and sit in the sub-conscience for him to weigh up.

I knew exactly where he had been. Trust had to be maintained and that meant a little marker without pursuing it.

But it was that chip shop where everything changed. Late February at teatime near a beach, he showed his hand.

We had been walking near the coast when suddenly around school kicking-out time, he spied a couple of youths and perhaps spurred on by his visit to The Midlands suddenly threw me the bait I had been waiting for.

Looking back and reading between the lines, the visit must have upped his game and rekindled the him of old and those predatory possibilities ahead. My instinct told me he was preparing. We were building to something. And I had his trust. In me, he saw the facility. That is why fish and chips led me to a defining moment.

'I like the look of that in there,' he said.

'I *like* fish and chips,' I replied as blandly as I had in the gay bar. I didn't even look in. I just carried on walking.

'No, those two schoolboys,' he blurted it out.

It was the first time he had been blunt. He was looking for a reaction –

confirmation that I was in, seeking re-assurance as we paused to linger outside while the boys ate inside.

They looked around thirteen years old in their uniform. His face said it all – delight at what might be on offer and relieved that he had put it out there.

He asked me what I thought.

I had to remember my default position. I had previously set my make-believe stall out as seven to twelve but not declared my hand with him:

'On a par,' I said. 'But they might be a bit younger.'

There it was done. He had finally engaged and I so had I knowing it was safe to do so.

'I wasn't quite sure,' he said always guarded but less tense.

'I wasn't quite sure either,' I smiled.

I knew that now was the moment. He began to drop in references to boys more and more. Only when their guard is down will you see their true colours. It will never be in a police interview weeks down the line because they have done their offending then and are facing charges. For now, you are their support so they are not worried. Mindful yes, but they are safe.

From this moment, everything changed. Every boy was an object. Every individual became an innuendo. But we were both using each other. It could only ever be a strange relationship. I had to re-engage.

I was always switched on but now we were at a new level where the tests would come again. New tests too. The patience and stress of getting to this stage meant that the pressure increased. I had unlocked a door that I had been prizing open over months. Everything changed in an instant. I could not have it slammed in my face. Of course, I was elated inside but my professional guard kicked back in.

I needed the evidence for the debriefing and I knew next time that we met, he would have been analysing all of this and we could go one step back before we went two forward. He could yet become more meticulous and more dangerous. He could go guarded again. It wouldn't take much to flush me out. I had to remember to keep re-introducing my mum to the point that it was natural for *him* to do so. When that happened, that level of total acceptance was also a given.

I was nearly there.

'What do you think of *him*?' became a routine question as he tried to hone in on exactly what I liked.

I knew exactly who he was and what he wanted from the intelligence but now, crucially I also knew it in character. The two parallel time zones of what was known and what I was allowed to know having learnt it from him were meeting. I had notes and I had it in my head. Now it was real. And behind the scenes it was a green light to proceed.

The test was on and it was always a game. I was trusted but I would have to go through new levels of engagement. He was building towards the network where I would have to prove myself all over again but without whom he could not fulfil his obscenities devoid of transport or alibi.

If it comes to it, I felt I was in control. However, he had the wild card of the network. I had him in my pocket but I did not know how what lay ahead. My head told me that he would definitely endorse me with them to achieve his own aims but then I still had to be accepted. I remembered Wales and the former army officer.

I also felt that he had been 'honest' up to this point. That is to say that I couldn't fault what he had shared with me, even if it were not the whole story. He never told me that he had been abusing anybody and there was no definitive evidence up to this point that he was re-offending.

However, it was clear that he was making moves and that train trip to The Midlands was out of the ordinary but not extraordinary in that it was something he had probably done in his previous incarnation before his incarceration.

I had given him the whiff of freedom to enjoy the stench of abuse. Now, I needed to follow the scent. He had gone alone and bought a train ticket. He knew I could have taken him. For now, he had paid his own way when it was in character to get someone else to do so. That was hugely significant because it would have been easier to use me for a freebie. There was a reason why he went alone.

It was time to revisit my line about the computers. I waited two weeks after the chip shop to drip-feed it in and test the water.

I needed to orchestrate a way in. And for the first time, we began to engage three other law enforcement agencies and would be reliant on their co-operation. This was expanding and it was time to bring them in. I needed to find that common denominator, keep focussed on the main target yet find a way to be part of that group whatever it consisted of. He may well have been talking to these people before the train trip. It is probably naïve to assume that just because he made me aware of it, it did not mean it started then. More likely, it was the first time he felt he could tell me.

If it led to a meeting, of one or all of them or just a phone call, it was my best chance.

Plus – he owed me a favour. I had covered for him for his trip. Now he needed to get me there too.

'I'm not comfortable with the PC,' I planted the seed. '*So* many people get caught.'

I had the confidence to air that language now given the fish and chip shop. I was also wary as it reminded me again of the officer in Wales who gave me nothing when others put it on the table.

The difference was plain here though. Then, I was dealing with a group to get to an individual. Now, it was the other way around.

'I know someone,' Edwin replied.

Bingo.

'I might need a bit of convincing,' I played weak.

'I will have a word for you.'

Our relationship was cemented.

'I appreciate he might be busy. Is it worth it?' I backtracked hoping he would seize on my hesitation.

And then he bit.

'You *must* give 'so and so' a call,' he offered.

This was a double-edged sword. He was taking me to the next level innocently whilst behaving as though there was nothing at risk. He knew whom he was putting me in touch with and where it might lead. I was his taxi and he thought I was one of them.

It was the moment we were waiting for.

18

It was time to talk to the psychologist Tom again. He knew little but more than most. We had openness and a good dialogue. He listened well without the need for operational detail, focussing instead on the mental energy that the longest game of cat and mouse required for this to come to fruition.

I had worked Edwin since that encounter on the bus. The team had been trailing him long before. My window of opportunity had been through the eye of a needle and I had knocked back his own advances several times. It was slow and painstaking, getting to know him whilst peddling the lie of my friend whom he had rarely seen except for three hours on the second visit, but somehow whose story he had bought. We had walked and talked. I had covered every inch of what there was to see in the North and I had replayed it all several times every time. My apprehension at rejecting him became an awareness that I had left a certain mystique as to what I was into.

'I hope you are not offended,' I had told him often. 'I want to be friends.'

Nor had I wanted him to be embarrassed and he wasn't. Ultimately, we had a relationship in a world where he could count on few legitimate people and my knock back was nothing compared to the world he lived in and some of the riskier places he frequented.

Why had he persisted with the *relationship* when there was no such relationship to speak of? It was simple, I was that alibi and I had transport and, in that fish and shop moment, we both declared our hand and he felt safe to pursue. It didn't matter anymore if he believed the cover story. Perhaps, he understood it as my way of flagging up what I wanted too.

I was mindful of George and Tom's advice to build in breaks. I was never all over him, so when weeks came like Christmas, I would re-charge my batteries well aware that gaps help to create your story. If you see or talk to somebody like this every day, you dry up. It had been entirely natural and paced perfectly.

But we were about to go into overdrive and that's why I had gone to see Tom. I knew that the process could start at a moment's notice. I had no idea when. Edwin had indeed facilitated the call to help me with my computer ignorance. This was my in:

'I really appreciate your time,' I flattered once again obeying the golden rule. They are an expert and need respect.

Of course, the voice at the end of the phone was very guarded. I couldn't know how many times my scenario had played out in the past when someone had attempted to introduce a third party to the group but I had witnessed that vetting all over again mentality in Wales.

'I'm apprehensive about computers,' I said.

He talked me through some basics and I allowed the detail to add to my confusion.

'I don't mind coming down to see you. It would be good to talk in person,' I finally asked after some time on the phone.

This was the test.

A week later, I got a call back.

'Why don't you come down?' the same man offered.

'I'll come with Edwin,' I replied instantly knowingly that it was probably unlikely that they would entertain me without but aware too that it verified our friendship. He had probably spent the previous week in conference over me. I counted on Edwin having endorsed me. This was now not the same as the army officer.

We mooted a couple of dates and I assured them politely that I did not want to distract anybody and then I played my bland get out of jail card again.

'I have care issues,' I said. 'But I'm sure we can sort something out.'

I told them I was grateful for the extensive knowledge and only they could help me learn more. Today, it was difficult to see why they might let me in but two factors were on my side. They loved that control that I handed them, and Edwin, in his own desperation to extend his lies to his probationers, *must* have told them that I was a good guy, that I was safe, that I was the one person that they could trust.

All I had to do now was to find that particular day when we could all meet – and I had no idea how many people *all* meant. I had to wait for them so I continued to hang around with Edwin without even mentioning it beyond that I hoped to hear from his associates soon. I knew that I was being vetted by others.

The operation was now gathering momentum at a pace and that meant meetings to discuss the 'What if?' scenario. Plans in your head needed to be short and to the point. Knowing your roles was vital. Nothing should be left to chance. You drill for a child being there and for not. You talk through recovery and your own exit strategy. Would there be a good time to come out of the role? That would be a last resort, assuming failure.

But at all costs, protect the child. Everything else was secondary. Whatever the pressure, the morality and ethical stance could not be shifted and it is all on your shoulders. Discussions were intense. Everybody knew the rules. But it might just be a computer lesson after all.

Now three weeks later, it was the night before the meet and I couldn't sleep. This was different. My gut told me we were building towards something – that the lesson might not last long. I was excited, thinking we were now moving into a network and the chances of meeting some associates could open other doors and we might get some sort of a result. I was also tense. This was way past bigger than Wales. It had momentum. The job could either be coming to an end but I didn't know what that conclusion would or more likely I would have to start all over again with these new acquaintances and remain on the maximum alert that I remember everything I have disclosed to Edwin.

I prepared myself that this meant I would have to justify myself all over again. It was different to Wales introducing Mr Big from Thailand because it was unlikely that we would have gone to Asia and that free spirit would be hard to track. Now, I was heading to The Midlands knowing that some intelligence was already in place for what lay ahead.

Once again, I recalled my training and re-focussed on how I dealt with indecent images that might be lurking on someone's computer. We were extremely confident that the only way Edwin could know this network, had to be through the sharing of child pornography or through prison circles. Their spheres of influence were small. It was entirely predictable that they came full circle and that anyone claiming to be a computer expert was using that skill to conceal what Edwin and the few people he knew were all into.

I lay there awake the night before, replaying every conversation. This is partly what Tom meant about the exhaustion. I analysed that scene on the bus over and over. I tried to remember the facial expressions and the nuances from outside the chip shop. I asked myself questions that I couldn't possibly answer as I asked myself if I had let my own guard down at any point.

I had to back myself that I had got to this stage alone with great support waiting in the wings. One man had entrusted me and he was now doing the same to his friends.

I didn't know any of the people's names I was about to meet. I had two genuine concerns. How could I prevent being given something and being raped? This is a genuine fear that when you are in their company such predators will and can turn into a sexual frenzy and some are very sordid in their sexual ways. What would I do if a child was introduced into the room? My responsibility always had to be that child even if that child had some sort of awareness of what was going on.

Save one child.

I didn't even know where we were going. I just knew that after our planning the previous day, we had established the key words that would trigger our exit strategy. That meeting showed it was now very serious and that this was bigger than even I knew. The paedophile unit and other forces had their meetings with operational heads and the Surveillance Team. Separate briefings kept it low key and focused but it was becoming complex. I suspect they knew more than me and on a different level. What I had which they didn't was his character in my head.

When I finally surfaced after the worst sleep ever, I had to pick Edwin up as early as possible to comply with his parole conditions. That meant from outside a railway station around half past nine. I was driving an ordinary vehicle with no obvious signs of it belonging to the police or showing modifications. I was wearing the tech from the off and that meant the need to orchestrate breaks but they would also help to detect mood swings and changes in behaviour. I had surveillance following me in various sequences so whilst I couldn't do anything other than let their journeys take their own course, a brief respite would enable them to re-group if required.

I had said goodbye to Julie who knew the importance of what I was going to be doing. She would worry about home. I needed to do the job. My emotions were mixed – apprehensive but confident. I was comfortable with Edwin, but the other or others only existed in terms of that phone call, so ahead lay the unknown.

I now had two to three hours to kill on the motorway. It was possible that I could be about to witness some dirty tricks I had not foreseen. This man I had known for a few months whose guard appeared to be down might suddenly overturn that evident vulnerability and reveal he had been playing me all the time. I had to drive, make conversation, watch the road with one eye in my rear mirror for my tail without knowing who it was but trusting that it was all there. Then there would be breaks where I would need to call something in and he may choose to do the same.

After the cagey way that we arrived here, this should have been the simplest exercise driving down a motorway to the end game. But it was now more than ever that I had to be wary, living in the moment worrying about what lay ahead and recalling still every last detail knowing that it would fall under fresh scrutiny in the next few hours.

It was time to hit the motorway and head towards the Midlands area.

19

The operational team knew the address. I had little more than 'Midlands area'.

'If we are running late I may have to call Mum,' I reminded him early of my well-established position.

I knew exactly where my first stop would be and drove steadily towards it. I would get as far as I could without compromise.

We chatted, left the radio on at a half volume to fill a void without it being a distraction, and had moments of silence. He was chatty and then not. There was no specific talk – no replaying of how we first met or testing me about the chip shop. It was the same as it ever was.

Anything could change in the blink of an eye. I was waiting for a twist in our conversations, but apprehensive as to what I was walking into but it remained a typical non-event of a car journey, except I knew within he was on tenterhooks with excitement. He was about to be off the leash. I was cautious to be consistent to the character I had always been, wary that I was driving and this was an unpredictable scenario but acutely conscious that I was providing a commentary to my ops team for the immediate mission that would protect me, the public and whoever unwittingly lay ahead.

The line is very difficult to straddle. It was important nobody got ahead of themselves. My brain was constantly splitting across all the necessary aspects of the character, the recall, the technical, the journey and whatever was to come. I remained calm but I was facing the maximum amount of mental stress, second only in stomach-churning anxiety to that moment in court just five minutes before they call your name to give evidence. No matter how many times you have been there every time feels like the first time. For this there were no precedents.

In the silences, my mind would drift to the traffic, occasional glances in the rear to spot anyone in the convoy but it was better that I knew less. I had total confidence that they were following. You had to let it go. Doing this work without the silent trust is impossible. At our operational and technical meetings the previous day, we had drilled and fine-tuned every likely scenario and how to deal with it – as much as you possible could.

In the miles ahead there remained that one variable – the public.

It was important to not over-stop. Flashback to Wales when I made two visits to the toilet in quick succession. Realistically, once we had pulled in, I would have to try to leave it for at least another hour.

'At the next services, I had better call the carer,' I stuck to the script. Edwin barely flinched. It was just part of our dialogue. 'I am now going to call the carer,' I re-iterated as I turned off the engine.

I was spelling it out to him, cementing that story.

There was no concern I might lose him at the toilets, behind a slot machine, or in the melee queuing for fast food. I had eyes all around me and he needed the ride. He couldn't do a runner and get far with his parole hours. His own common sense told him that he needed a lift home too. After all, where do you go to when you flee a motorway service station?

I sat in the cubicle of the toilet and changed the tapes. I hid them and then bought some computer magazines. Remember – that was the purpose of my visit.

I called work briefly just to check in. There was nothing to report and no unusual behaviour. Everything was eerily on track.

Then Edwin got back in the car.

'I might have a surprise for you later,' he stunned me.

'I like surprises,' I replied.

'We may have a boy visiting the flat.'

'What a surprise,' I feigned delight.

I had considered that he might come back to the vehicle with a new request like a change of location. In your planning, you would believe that he would use the break in the same way that we would.

I smiled back, understanding the parameters of what he was saying but not the specifics. But he suddenly had control and also put me in a tricky position as we set off. I couldn't stop again any time soon and I needed to get this back. I re-considered our exit strategy – get out at all costs if compromised. I was far from there yet but when you are hit with that bolt out of the blue you have been waiting for, your mind spins into fast forward, then you get dragged back into the present.

He wore a flippant smile – excitement in his eyes as he delivered these words. He came to life. Seconds before I had been telling base that there was nothing to report, and that it was all going to plan and now my mind was racing ahead as to what and where and who this means whilst concentrating on the road, and then once it has taken a couple of minutes to sink in, I retrace my reactions back to the moment he said it, wondering if I gave the game away or if all that training at looking at those sterile images and learning not to react but then to perform a little had served me well. That is what I mean by going into fast forward and being pulled back slow-mo to the moment.

It was horrific. His one short sentence told me I was in. Of course, it said danger but there would never be this job without risk. All it made me do was question how I had come across and wonder how to call this in.

I think I didn't react externally. My physique hadn't changed. The journey continued as normal. There was no sign that I had responded out of character. Inside, that stomach churned a little more. The enclosed space of the car on the way to such an important job made it even more excruciating. There was no George, there was no break for dessert, there was no cheap hotel reception – this was it. Just the two of us with him holding all the cards until I could claw it back.

Within moments, my confidence was not only restored, it rose. I saw the bigger picture. He had shared the end game with me. Once I had been his alibi to get that train to the Midlands. Now we were going together. I realised in fact that I had passed another test. He could have used that service station himself to feign sickness or find an equivalent of my carer, but instead he opened the door. I reverted to my calm, knowing that we were doing very well. It is hard to analyse as you go but that was my conclusion.

Operations were like a coiled spring, waiting on my every move. I knew not to do anything in panic. I was grateful that I had signposted that we might make an unscheduled stop. That moment had to be sooner or later now.

He had control but only briefly. He handed it back as he sort this re-assurance that I was pleased. I hadn't flinched. I had given him a green light and he was checking this was what I wanted. He had delivered his line almost destructively with timing and superiority but I seized it back as soon as he double-checked with me.

At the front of my mind was one thing. I needed to make that second stop. All the plates were spinning in the car. I had to get out and make a call once more. For clarity in my head, and to relay the information. I couldn't do it immediately. I needed him rock solid on side. If I was challenged later, he would be my buffer. Timing was everything for the trust of our relationship.

I did the only thing I could do. I thought about the carer and turned it back to him.

I had let the surprise die down and let the music play a little before I started to feign concern.

'What do you think I should do?' I asked. 'I can see this day over-running already. Shall I put another call in or leave it for a bit?'

I hoped he would take this in no other way other than that I was now even keener for that surprise. I was showing my commitment to whatever it was. I was buying us both time. Surely, he wasn't thinking I was calling it in.

I took a risk and made the second stop just 29 miles later. I wasn't comfortable with this at all but I decided I had no choice. I made that emergency break.

'They might already be committed,' I told him well aware of the potential of a schedule clash for my non-existent carer.

I then got out of the vehicle and within a safe distance made the call. I knew I was probably out of stops now. This had to count.

'There's a suggestion there may be a child,' I spoke very slowly and deliberately to the Ops team.

Then I repeated it so there could be no doubt.

I knew that coiled spring had just bounced into overdrive.

It was one thing being told that this might be on and taking a moment to digest it. It was another to call it in and knowing that it was all systems go whilst you had to remain in character.

Suddenly my heart was racing again with the implications of what I had relayed. This time I walked slowly back to the car and bluffed. 'That was close,' I told Edwin. 'It was a good job I did phone. The carer was planning to go out.'

I needn't have worried. He was too far ahead of himself in excitement and I knew that if he left the car, he was being followed and might make another call.

He may have needed that break too or at least, a diversion at some point so would have taken whatever stop I engineered. Was he calling it in every time I was? I felt we were back on track. Control was even. Then he seized it again.

'We might have a boy,' he delivered, matter-of-factly.

'That sounds nice,' I replied.

Then paused. It was the same sensation. Fast forward into overdrive, a million beats per second then step back and analyse how I had reacted. Follow that with the previous reminder that I was doing well and that he wasn't testing me. I was already in. He was just taking me closer. The only thing in the way was if I had radiated disinterest. I had passed all his tests some time ago.

I wasn't expecting further revelation.

Then my mind started again. He knew this when he announced a surprise. He was pacing out the distribution of the information, giving it to me in bits. Not only did we have what we believed to be present in the network but we also now had a live situation where a child was at risk and could already be there. As I drove towards the lair, the boy might be laying naked on the bed. Or it could be a bluff. I reminded myself of why we were doing this. And I couldn't stop thinking it over again.

'There might be a boy coming to flat,' he repeated three or four times in his excitement and to check I was in. I still did not have a final destination.

Then we were back to business as usual exchanging pleasantries and small talk as the traffic got heavier heading to the Midlands. The mental trick of sensing what you were driving towards but not knowing where it was intensified the tension within me. I had not made any assumption as to the destination but you really wanted to know. At any moment, he could say that it was 'just here on the left' and indeed probably would, and then I could be thrust into a scenario with new people – probably the guy I spoke to briefly on the phone about the computer, with all my recalls being tested whilst protecting any minor and preserving the evidence.

I focussed again on what George had told me all those years ago. Save one child.

Clearly, we were getting closer. Dual carriageways had replaced motorways. Then the variable of traffic played its hand.

I spied one of the surveillance vehicles that I knew to be one of ours. In a split second, I had looked up and saw it *above* me on the flyover. We were going under and they were going up. I knew this was wrong and not an elaborate decoy in a complicated convoy tail. That part of the UK road network can take you off anywhere – to the West Country, to London, Oxfordshire or into the back roads of the Black Country.

It played with my head.

'What's he doing?' I asked myself without trying to give off negative body language. I knew he had taken the wrong turn even though I didn't know where I was going and could not identify the individual drivers. It was too far out of the way.

All the time Edwin was giving me directions, honing me in on the final location. I had to let it go and assume that I was still being sufficiently protected and that he was a skilled enough biker to re-join the group. I don't think Edwin caught my rolling eyes of disbelief.

Then he suddenly uttered those words.

'It's here,' he said after the dual carriageway became a minor road.

And it was that quick.

His own guard was down too. He had no concept of losing a tail, and even though he didn't know he had one, most people in his position would take you round the houses as precaution. Instead, we just pulled up opposite the flat and he gestured that we had arrived.

Tailing is at its most difficult, of course, when the lead vehicle is about to pull up and is driving on back roads where visibility is not so far ahead as it is with motorways. Local knowledge of cul-de-sacs can really count when the car you are tracking is about to stop. You don't want to find yourself in a dead-end street with nowhere to turn.

Edwin was not sufficiently security conscious or a driver himself. He made it easy for the convoy. I had a rough idea of their presence without knowing much more of anything that would alert me.

'Is my car okay here?' I asked. Not that it mattered.

'Yeah, fine,' he replied.

His mind was already out of the vehicle.

'This is it.' We're here. 'We'll get the lift.'

He spoke the words of a man who had been here before. I know understood that I had possibly given him the alibi once before.

I took a deep breath and remembered a final time why we were here.

Edwin and I had different agendas.

Mine was to save one child.

20

He pressed the button for the thirteenth floor. Unlucky for some. It took an eternity for the lift to descend and even longer to go up.

I tried to remain cool. My tech was running. Edwin was my gatekeeper. The tower blocks reminded me of those early days around Stoke Newington. The smell of stale sweat and urine never left you. This was it. No going back or having second thoughts. You are focussed. Now it is the unknown seeing new people not knowing who or how many. Despite the butterflies, this was not the time for self-doubt. It is time to trust your ability.

I looked at Edwin's 6'4. In his full-size out of the car, his strapping build struck me again. I was familiar with it of course, but I now feared his friend or friends could be the same. One I might handle, a group would be a problem. At some point, I could be physically tested.

The car seemed a long time ago, even though we had just parked up. Tension does that to your perception of how long something lasts.

I had told him on the journey down that I really hoped I would learn a few things about computers today. *That* seemed days ago. Yet his timeline was running at twice the speed with a different adrenaline. He was excited in the lift, couldn't wait to exit it whereas I could easily wait another minute.

Then he knocked on the door – a door which would soon shut on us imprisoning us all in this secret world.

It began.

'Hi, how was your journey?'

The new small talk began. We were in.

On the left, I spotted the toilet; ahead was a small hall. In the corner also on the left I could see the living room. There was a fireplace to the side and a settee. The kitchen was in another corner, and then I spotted it scanning my eyes back, trying to work out where my exit was.

In the living room stood a table and on that table was a computer. This was to be the first prop. I had only one way out unless I wished to abseil and that way out was exactly the way I had come in. It was the first thing you looked for.

'Cup of tea or a ham sandwich?' said the guy in the room.

I declined the pleasantries. There was no way I was eating anything made from their dirty hands. The new friend *looked* grubby, creepy and skinny with greasy hair. He tried to dress young but was gaunt-looking in his 40 s.

Around me, there was no evidence here of what I was looking for. Just the computer on the table and whatever was on it. For no reason that I can offer, he also had a budgie which he let free around the room. I did not want that interrupting proceedings or squawking so loudly that it wrecked the tape.

On my decline, the budgie had my share of the ham sandwich.

It was all that grubby.

It was time to be gracious and ask for help. I wanted the guy to know again that I was thankful for his time and that I really did not have a clue about computers.

He began the process of going through everything very slowly. Edwin just watched while he talked. His eyes were fixed on me judging my reaction. He had the power and control back.

Then it happened. We got onto pictures and he pulled up an image. He asked me what I liked. It was borderline legal. This was the start. Another hurdle to overcome. The first test in the flat.

'What do you think?' he asked me.

This was clever stuff, starting with a mild yet all but illegal image to see if he could take me further. The game had started. What would be next?

'I don't know if they are under age there,' I answered.

They certainly did.

I see today as I saw it then. In clear daylight in my mind. In real time.

The picture changes. The examination had begun but he needed some reassurances before progressing. I could sense that the chat was deliberate and my responses were being listened to.

Every word that I now say, how I say it and my body language is being assessed and analysed. The man does not give me chance to draw breath, hitting me with his interpretations and of course wanting answers that make sense to a paedophile. Out of the corner of my eye, Edwin's role is to observe me, saying little just the odd laugh and a grunt of approval at what I am being shown.

I am on high alert. I sense no respite. The testing is going to be constant and if I survive one layer, then we will be going deeper and deeper into this murky world.

The images start again and the severity of them is clear to see. I *know* that I am passing the test but that now this is going to be one long haul. Over and over… each one repetitive and yet the image would remain on the screen. I can't look away. I have my method in my mind. The image does not exist. Back to my original training.

The hurdles keep coming. I am progressing, unaware when this is going to end.

Next on the screen I see young boys masturbating and ejaculating and sexual abuse right before my eyes. Edwin is saying nothing. His focus remains locked on me. His credibility is on the line as much as mine. Despite the talk between us we had never gone this far. There was not any opportunity given his parole – until now.

'What happens if you don't want anyone else seeing a picture?' I asked naively. 'If the phones rings and you are distracted then someone walks in…?'

He shows me how to hide a picture and I marvel at his expertise.

Then he elaborates.

'I've got something in place if somebody comes in. I press one button and it's lost.'

Then he looks at me almost asking for acknowledgement of his expertise.

'It's lost,' he says. 'But it is still on the hard drive.'

This was thinking ahead of its time in the 1990 s.

Now I begin to think that if I have to call this in, I must tell anybody not to touch the computer. That old and creamy device was now a vital piece of evidence. He was telling me his technique and effectively sharing that he had already hidden plenty.

'You look after your Mum, don't you?' he asks.

Edwin had done me proud in promoting my cover story.

'Yeah – she has a carer,' I tell him what he already knows. He wouldn't have *not* got everything out of Edwin before allowing me to come.

'Depending on what happens today, I might have to call her,' I flag up that I am anticipating more images and people but that I have my excuse ready to go.

'Yeah, he might have to,' Edwin confirms.

Then he is back to the screen.

I am analysing myself whilst acting the role. Are my reactions appropriate? Am I showing the correct levels of enthusiasm? If they start to touch themselves, do I join in? I know what I am doing. That is not for me. I have my excuses in my head. They will be suspicious. There may be pressure.

Whatever you do it is not about now it is about you at the court months later justifying why you did it. Everything has to be measured. You cannot force the issue. You must not get lost in the moment.

I stick my tongue out at the screen as if I was excitedly licking the monitor. I have practised this.

'What does this button do?' I ask when I need a sideshow. With Mr Thailand I was prepared to spill a drink, now I can delay with any number of buttons in front of me.

But there is no stopping the two of them. The owner of the flat gestures me towards his fireplace.

'Wait a minute,' he pauses loving the control that his drama exudes.

It looks unused. Then I see why.

He puts his hand up the left-hand side.

It emerges with a wad of discs.

Wow – I really am being given the keys to the castle. His giddiness and naivety are running away with him. He flicks through the lot, almost playing with them bringing them down one by one. They are all indecent images. There are around 1,000 to sit through.

The content is getting more and more severe – the pressure intense and made worse by the fact that he is getting comfortable with me. I keep my guard. Now is not the time to let it slip.

If anything, the number helps me stay in the zone. I am not now being tested as to my reaction. We have passed that. Instead, he is simply showing off as if it were an initiation ceremony and I was being welcomed to the fold.

'You're one of us then?' he finally comes out and says it.

'I might be,' I mumble hesitantly and in a very guarded manner.

I am not sure why I did that. You never quite wanted to say it out loud nor did you want to illicit crime under false pretence. Equally, if you were genuinely shy and new to this scenario and with your security up as many paedophiles were, then that might be the correct tone to give off.

I am sure about one thing – that I don't want to give him anything I don't need to. But it is enough. He is comfortable. His guard drops, interspersed only by the occasional grunt from Edwin whom I had never heard so quiet ...and the parrot. The flat owner tells me he has been to Amsterdam and knows The Blue Boy and Why Not inside out. This is my moment and I take him to task when he describes the building as only having two storeys when I know there is that secret third floor with all the cubicles. It is my chance to put all that research into practise, detailing every last detail of coming from the train station and singling out cafes pressing home every piece of knowledge and furiously contesting with him the layout of this seedy bar. He relents so it looks like *his* credibility is questioned in front of his mate. Mine goes up a notch. I simply couldn't have carried it off it we hadn't done the work.

We all begin to talk very openly about the images on the screen. Edwin analyses a picture; the flat owner does the same then they both want my feedback. I know this is all it takes to get their levels of frenzy heightened and I need it for the benefit of the tape. I also want to be clear to those listening how many people are in the flat. As it stands there are three – and a budgie.

Then a mobile rings. This must have been semi-choreographed along the lines of 'if you don't hear from me within a specific time, then assume it is on and you can call to come to the flat.'

I didn't want to be inquisitive but my head was telling me this.

'One of our friends is coming,' I am told. 'They will be here soon.'

We are about to be four.

I could have used this opportunity to make a call myself but I don't need to so there is no need to waste an unnecessary life. I think the scenario is clear to those who are listening in.

But now I have to contend with our new friend and with that I know the process will begin again. It would be time to pass further tests and of course the examination of myself will be repeated all over again. The importance of recalling everything I have said and indeed have merely implied is vital. It only takes one to put a spanner in the works and sow that seed of doubt.

Here we go again.

The new arrival is slimmer, thinner and in a long coat. That used to be the stereotypical image but it applies today. He comes in and sits next to me and becomes even more intense than the first guy. Was this how it always worked – you entered according to a ladder of hierarchy? Logic, and Wales seemed to suggest so.

It gives them a chance to up the filth on the screen, re-appraise me as we go through much of the same again and of course, play tricks on my mind as I try to recall what I had said to the previous guy. Time is dragging on – there was no quick pay off here. Occasionally, Edwin would chip in with a question but still mostly watches. He thought he knew every detail about me. The truth is I had shared very little. He was the guy who sold me to them. It was not the other way around.

It was clear that one piece of training rang very true. They were always interested in meeting like-minded people and that was how I had been allowed to infiltrate. Their fear was journalists but even though I was still being worked out, I was mostly past that point. If I didn't slip up, it would be fine.

Whilst trying to evaluate my own recall, I was also living in the future. This was going somewhere, but to what point? A couple of hours in, preserving the disks was my priority. If the much-promised boy turned up, then making him safe was the only option. And from time to time in all this intensity, we would break for a chat and a cup of tea. An act of the most ordinary normality amidst such a stressful and frenzied hive of activity. It was as though they needed the break too.

Then it would begin again as though it was literally starting afresh. Images I had already seen together with new ones and the same technique over and over again. And if I thought they were watching for my reactions before, now they are really looking at me.

Two skills were at play here. Firstly – introduce a break so I might relax and be caught off guard when we begin again. Very simple. It happens in sport often that after a short delay or a half time, it seems a completely different ball game. I used the same techniques. Secondly, if they re-run images I have already seen with someone and I am inconsistent to my previous reactions then the game is up.

Then just as we are getting going again, the flat owner retreats to the kitchen. I see this now as the place where the phone rings and then I hear one end of the conversation.

'How long will you be?'

This was getting even more serious. Just when I was getting used to the mentality and the role-playing, number four is on his way. This was the ultimate test but there was still no reason for me to alert anyone. I did not need to make the mistake of reading more arrivals with bigger reputations as more danger until that threat is genuine.

I have no awareness of time. That door opens again. A new test. Each of them is making a decision on me. 'I think he's OK, what do you think?' was the thought process. By allowing the next one in, they had satisfied themselves that I was fine and they individually were comfortable but just wanted to pass it on for further re-assurance.

I assumed I was working my way through the hierarchy too. Edwin was therefore somewhere near the bottom. I couldn't know if and when the process would be complete but I had to back what he had said in the car. There might be a surprise. There might be a boy. I had to work on the basis that I was passing every test so far and that at some point they too had built their excitement levels up and would need their release of tension. I backed myself to stay in the role and be patient. I was doing well and it should be today.

The new guy takes over. Arrival Number Four is now sat in front of me on a stool. Number three is next to me. They are all crowding around me, looking at me. I can feel their breath.

Their proximity is intimidating enough but I had been here before and this time nobody is touching me and getting close to my wire. If only they had, they would know but this was a different scrutiny to Wales. I just sensed that if I survived the re-interrogations of my reactions then their need for their sick pleasure would be their downfall. Mr Big for Thailand was only ever playing me. This was different. These guys were vetting me so they could play with something else – as tasteless as that sounds.

In my head, I feel there are still more of the group coming in. They must have been happy with me. They would have not incriminated themselves by arriving otherwise. They would have called it off. Now the language has gone up a gear too. Those early simple exchanges about how to hide an image – any picture at all – have been replaced with graphic discussion about how to break the young ones in.

They have a style of communicating that is nothing short of offensive yet always ups the language to almost goad the next person to express an opinion. The tone of their voices would change – intensity became giggling.

A new image on the screen would see their personalities change in their entirety as they began to talk about them. Predatory and sick, waiting to pounce, hungry for more... all the time looking to see what you might give away.

Boys of around five years old are now on the monitor. I continue to stick my tongue out. The more repetitive the process becomes, the more intense it does too. I couldn't for one moment think I have done all this before, this is a walk in the park. No, it is worse. The parallels with police work were not lost on me. We too would often ask the same questions over and over again to spot chinks in the armour. They were doing exactly the same to me.

My head is full of several layers of recall – from the entire history of Edwin and I, to today and the journey down almost fading into the memory to the immediate of the last few hours and we are now four to five hours in. Broadly speaking my sense of time has gone. I am just concentrating minute to minute.

Number Five enters. A lad in his early twenties, his standing within the group seemingly low down despite him being one of the later arrivals. You sense that, but you cannot belittle this person.

He is still in the group of trusted men and in truth I remain the newest arrival in their world. His eyes are all over me, weighing me up looking at other members of the group for their reaction.

There is one more. Number Six. This is good despite the process re-setting itself once more. It is obvious that he *is* respected and has that air of seniority. I take this as massive. He is ultimately going to be the decision maker. That means this might be the end of the line.

On his say, it seemed, the afternoon might proceed or hang by a precarious thread where it just self-destructed and we had to extract awkwardly. As he enters with everyone bouncing off each other, constantly with eyes peeled, I tell myself to protect and narrate the evidence again. I know this of course but his presence seems to signal the end game.

He barely speaks – perhaps just 12 words – adding to the intensity and drama. Beware the silent assassin. He who does not speak uses his skills to watch. I do not lose sight of the fact that whilst I took him as a sign that we might crack this cell tonight, I knew it also is a message to the others that they too might get what we had come for. All the signs were there for the network in the room *and* myself. We just interpret them differently.

Suddenly the pattern is broken. The focal point of the computer and the table are no more. For the moment, that reduces the tension but it had been a stress I could live with. You found a zone to manage it because it was the same all the time, just with new characters arriving.

'Oh look,' the flat owner stuns me. 'I'll show you my bedrooms.'

I repeat it back as a question so it is clear and that it is on his instigation.

'You'll show me the bedrooms?' I confirm.

But that stress that I was managing at the table is only relieved in an instant and the respite has short-term value because I am now dealing with a new test. I am away from the seat I have been glued to, comfortable there in my position and consistent in my demeanour and I now run the risk that I might show that strain lifting from my face whilst equally have to calmly radiate the message of 'yes please' to the bedroom. I had to show expressions that this was what I had come for without suddenly jumping out of character or expressing relief.

The most recent arrival was the green light. They know the signal. The quizzing in front of the images on screen and the mental analysis of me all around is over in its current form.

The flat owner gets me out of the room. I try to keep my ears peeled. It might be a distraction and an opportunity for rest of the group to assess what they have heard and seen.

New tests were beginning but so was fresh scrutiny.

It did not bear over-thinking beyond a professional capacity of what had gone on in here. Had they all also undertaken this vetting initiation with others in the past? It *felt* like they had a system that had been used previously. Perhaps some had not got this far but I am definitely gaining trust all the time. The bedroom is the next rung on the ladder. There is no reason to take me there if I am not now accepted and if it isn't to be a place where I am supposed to imagine its possibilities.

Had I ever seen anything like it? Definitely not. It is full of female dresses hung up in see-through plastic bag with female wigs scattered on the floor.

'Whose are they?' I ask.

Then I realise we were now moving at a rate of knots.

'We've got this boy,' I am told quite calmly. 'He is getting past his sell-by date.'

And I hear his tone rise to excitement.

'So we get him dressed up.'

Save one child.

'We have sex in the bath.'

I now had real context to George's words.

'We do it here too,' he points. 'He can take all that.'

I had the truth – a confession of the previous… or the greatest bravado on earth but I know it was the former.

George's words come back again. Save one child now means from further destruction. Like many, he has already suffered. We are unlikely to ever prevent an initial offence especially under the current legislation. The best we can hope for is to protect their future. This was always going to be damage limitation.

Things are moving fast.

'He might come to the flat, you know,' the owner tells me.

I interpret that as highly likely if I don't mess this up. It confirms what Edwin had intimated on the journey down. I have to stay focussed with new challenges ahead. I had done the hard work. I need to remember my basics – recall, and the technical whilst watching the language that those monitoring could interpret. Then I have to re-focus on avoiding nudity, harm to the boy and timing my extraction from the flat.

I feel calm. I realise only now looking back this was the ultimate in stress.

'Oh right, is he coming to the flat?' I ask trying to give off that nonchalant attitude.

'Yes, we're just waiting,' he adds.

Might had just become *will*.

He was getting me there in stages. The test continues but less gruelling. Every line is a chance for me to blow it and further confirmation to them that I am sound. This man had previously experienced his wicked way with 'the boy' but I was in no doubt that the profiling which saw these people wanting to be perceived as experts actually equalled control issues and whilst they were all here for the same thing, would also delight in the newcomer in me being the first to have a go. It was that kind of mentality. No concept of intimacy, just power and abuse.

My mind is racing. In reality, he had just given me the sign that I needed to play my reserve card. I am grateful I have not over-egged it.

'Oh right,' I began a couple of sentences later. 'I don't know if you remember but I might have to make a call to my carer about my Mum. I do hate to miss anything.'

This scenario had never let me done.

'Oh yes, that's fine,' he replies.

I think by now they are gone.

His mind is already ahead going into great detail about the bedroom which was nothing short of a horrible cesspit. It had only a mattress in it and the air was filled with a horrible stale smell. I noticed some sex toys such as vibrators. He could see that I had spotted them but that I made no comment. It was an obvious moment that did not really need any explanation. I am sure he visualised previous conquests as he shared me what he liked to do with the boys just as we re-entered the living room.

The atmosphere has changed.

'I hear the boy could be coming,' he announces.

One of the group had made a call from the kitchen.

Everybody's ears had pricked up.

'I think he is going to call when he's coming up the stairs,' one of the others chirps unable to contain himself, his voice rising an octave in the process.

For the first time, I know now it *is* going to happen. It is on. I witness reactions in front of me that I know they had all portrayed before. The tests are over. The guard is down. That final little chat in the bedroom when he went from 'might come' to 'we're just waiting' still had a tease about it but the game of bluff is up when the whole room becomes aware. I am now officially one of them and that means I need to make that call sooner rather than later.

It is time.

A phone rings. It is not mine.

'I'll be with you in a couple of minutes.' We all heard it. 'I'm just coming up the stairs.'

I need to make that call.

I am now ahead of myself. The final scenario is playing out in my head. I am concerning myself with the fact that the police have thirteen flights of stairs to mount.

It has to be the end. I am coming to the most critical moment. I can feel conclusion. Everything you plan and prepare for is now a reality. Except there is no text book.

The boy is coming. I have to make that call. It is now or never. I might not get another chance. I don't know what is going to happen or the involvement they have in mind for me but I will not be able to interrupt what is surely to come. I take the plunge.

The group are in a frenzy, high on pre-sexual anticipation. It is impossible to control what is going to happen next. I have to call it in. I will need to protect the child. I can certainly be holding onto one male but six men is a non-starter. My mind is racing. They are starting to really show their level of intent. The voice in my head is yelling at me to phone now. I pause and breathe. I gather my thoughts back before they run away. It is now.

'Do you mind if I just quickly call my carer?' I break their excitement. 'They do know I might be late.'

They have other things on their mind. Their guard is down. They don't even question.

I turn my phone on and take the few steps to the kitchen making sure they *can* hear me. Their eyes no longer trail me. Their focus is on each other's faces and most importantly, the door. I dial the number and pause. I wait to hear the voice at the other end.

Then I activate the key words:

'I am definitely going to be late, okay. I am going to be late, okay'. I deliver the line four times. 'I definitely will be late and I am sorry.'

These are the most important words. I repeat them so there is no doubt. They couldn't say the reception was dodgy or be any under illusions. There was no room for misinterpretation.

It is done. At the other end of the line the message is received with stunned silence. They have been waiting for my call all afternoon and then their phone springs into life. They are on tenterhooks too. They couldn't miss my call. It has meant simply watching patiently.

Then, after the silence, comes the double-take.

'Did he really just say what I think he said?' the call-handler questions my words.

'Yes, he said it another three times,' another confirms.

My stomach goes in the process. I am sure it is mutual.

If the boy comes in I have to protect him. I keep telling myself – it's all about the child. Save one child.

The excitement levels in the room are at fever pitch. One of them cannot stand it anymore and has gone to the toilet. They are almost screaming and shouting like a baying mob – for a lad they had described as past his sell-by date, itself an indication of how abusive they had been in that he was probably past his use and his best in their eyes and yet this sacrificial lamb is the way they will initiate me.

All the files I had read where I had learned their mantra that they loved children and that grooming was a term made up by the media just blew up in their face. This is obviously not affection. They are preparing for control, abuse and even in their hierarchy with me now at that bottom, that control and that abuse are plain to see.

It is well documented *now* that abusers were often abused themselves and those whom they then do the same to continue the cycle. There is nothing here to dispute this.

The frenzy steps out of control. Images are playing non-stop on the screen working them into an even more excited state. And all the time the budgie is still flying across the room and chipping in its monosyllabic two pennies worth. It provides a comic touch in a very tragic scene.

And then the noise stops. Everything falls quiet. Even the budgie.

We are finally on.

The doorbell rings.

21

The silence lasts maybe a second. Perhaps it is half a minute. It kills the noise in the room. It takes me aback even though I was conditioning my mind that it is coming. They use the silence to gawp at each other with expectation. I have to re-focus.

I am standing next to the computer in the living room. I have no idea as to what the boy looks like. My stomach churns. I have come this far, passed so many tests and now comes the final and ultimate examination. This is the only one that counts.

I look casually around. I try to *look* casual. I see all of them in the zone. No one is paying any particular attention to me anymore. The prize is about to enter the room.

Now time begins to run at those different speeds again. It stands still in that moment when the doorbell rings. Yet I know it is going at twice the pace on the Ops Team. That clock is now ticking too. I just don't know how long I have.

I have no choice but to be confident that there is no confusion over my words that they heard. The trust I had on the motorway that my tail was still there remains. I have to assume. I can't be distracted by that. I had been deliberate in my tone on the call. I had to let their side of events play out.

And then I see the boy.

The guy who had been mostly silent begins to laugh. The control is under the way. This is the love of children they so often talked about.

The noise goes back up.

Yet the boy enters with the flat owner whose arm is casually around his back. The boy is clam, unfazed by the hysterical laughter and frightening screams from the room.

He seems about twelve – slim with sort hair, blue jeans and clean trainers. He doesn't look like he had been to school. I would never know what hold they have on him that he comes on demand when he gets the call, as I have to assume he had done previously. He seems numb to abuse. There is no fear in his eyes because there is no look. The light has gone out. The look on his face I now understand as immune – all senses and sensitivities ripped out of him.

I would later learn that he had in fact been passed from group to group.

My task is as simple as it was complicated. I have to keep this scenario live but sterile. I have to find a way to time all of this to a heightened point of virtually caught in the act by the moment my colleagues bash down the door even though I do not how far away that moment was.

In the interim, I have to play a lead role.

'This is John,' one of the group tells the boy ushering him to me.

Whilst that is not my name, I never know his. I was not John and Edwin was not Edwin. Their so-called love of children is so disrespectful names are an irrelevance and he has been groomed so well that he does not ask any questions. Nor is there any apprehension in his body at all or any fear in his face. He just looks as though sex – once or multiple – is par for the course.

I have passed all their tests. They are about to offer me the ultimate reward in their eyes. They will wait, desperate to see me with the boy. What kind of love was that too that they all craved this poor poor lad but then are going to give him away to a relative stranger? This is abuse, control *and* entertainment.

The boy is now next to me. His arm is around my waist, my arm around his. We are locked. I now have control of the boy and he is unwittingly next to the computer with the men to my right. Both of us are now protecting the other important part of the operation. We need to save the computer. The disks are all over the place. When the police raid they will get lost or damaged. We must save the computer.

The group begin to focus on me. Hysteria subsides briefly and analysis takes over again, watching how I am reacting with the boy and pondering what I am going to do. The screams of encouragement and laughter rise once more. I am adding to the confusion by my actions. I am looking at the boy saying how nice he looks and talking for talking's sake. The boy remains calm and with control. That is the effect of the grooming process. It is now a normal scene that he recognises from previous occasions. The flat owner is right. He knows the buy. He will never make any disclosures to a third party because they have worked him well.

He had intimated that the boy was now passing his sell by date *but* still had uses and was in the process of bringing younger boys into the group. That was the level of abuse. They didn't really want him. But he served a purpose.

That clock ticks again. I have no idea if it is now minutes or much longer since I made that call. It obviously feels like the latter. I assume they are on their way. I had left it to the last possible minute.

It's all about the child. Save one child.

Nobody has touched him. It is a waiting game. Soon somebody will make the first move. It is odds on that that they will assign that role to me.

Outside I am unaware of the chaos that my team are embroiled in. The first set of officers find the lift is not working – that very same lift I had ascended in with Edwin with what I then thought was tension but which is unrecognisable from this stress. That adrenaline now seems miniscule. My colleagues' stress is different. They have to run the thirteen flights avoiding noise and attention though thankfully in the flat the volume is high and the spotlight is on the boy.

This is the wild card of life again. Why is that lift not working? I have none of these answers. Oblivious to this, all I can start to think as I wait is that they hadn't heard me. The equipment must have failed me. I have an obligation to protect this boy yet I don't know how long I have. I must hang on. I have to let the scenario play out and make the call myself if I bale and I must do so according to the ever-changing set of circumstances I am in and not because I perceive that five minutes has actually been an hour.

I resolve to delay as much as I can whilst masquerading as a man very much enjoying the moment. The budgie starts up again to add to the cacophony in the room. Alongside that, I am doing my best to provide commentary for the tape without over-doing it all the time, battling the voice in my head which is measuring time and taunting me as to where the back team are.

I know the group are looking at me thinking why hasn't he done anything yet. Yet equally the thrill is always in the chase and they are enjoying the show, but then there isn't one. There has to be a cut off time. The pressure for me to make a move on him accentuates but instead I just stand there holding him tight and he clings to me too.

My body and my mind are poles apart. The thought process is telling me to get out; yet the limbs are not moving. The physical me rightly defies the mental one. I stay put for as long as I can. I am making the boy safe. This will be the only time he walks out of this flat intact. That is my mantra as I slap down the thoughts of fleeing – but still they return.

I am doing well. I am in the home straight. This is the final piece of the jigsaw. I have to hold on and wait. I must believe and retain the faith that they are on the way.

This all started on a bus in the North of England. Months later you are in a flat in The Midlands and you have them. This is the groundwork in Wales and the research in Amsterdam. It's for all those images you viewed alone and learnt your reactions. It's for all the stuff you didn't bring home and it is all for the child. All this can be worth it to save one child.

I am so nearly there but what is my next move? I am not coming on to him. He grabs my shirt. I don't know if he recognises he might be safe for once. I don't know if our clench feels different and *safe* or if he is just waiting for it all to start.

He is gripping me tight. If he is immune to abuse then he won't recognise comfort either. The experts can deal with his thought process after, I reason.

Everybody is laughing in the room. I am a figure of fun and the boy is taunted. They *are* waiting for me to proceed. I see Edwin from the corner of my eye. He is totally in the zone loving every moment and egging me on. The others do not take their eyes off me.

I hope words will derail the process.

'What a lovely boy. You look nice. You're so slim,' I lied.

I recognise the haunted soul of the abused.

The clock continues to tick. I know I am now getting to the point where I have to make a choice. Something has gone wrong. I have to come clean. I am out of chances. I have taken this as far as I can. And they are taking too long.

We have enough on tape to prosecute under the laws of the day and we need go no further given that I cannot and will not sacrifice the boy to abuse for the sake of keeping the network live and leading me to the next sting.

That is the rule. We didn't work like that. I tell myself we have enough. It is too long now. The pretence is at its end. The others are beginning to look at each other.

Clarity. There is nothing left to do.

It is time to get the boy out of the flat.

22

I am out of time. I am making the decision to extract. I have hung on long enough. The door is not shut but neither is it locked from the inside. I am preparing the words and toying with how to maintain a grip of the boy whilst getting out of there fast.

I am now standing, still holding him. I will not let go.

My mind is racing …the boy, the tech, the images, the fireplace, the carer, the others in the room, the fish and chip shop, the bus journey, the …

Boom. Then it happened.

Six officers storm the door, banging it down. The noise is not so much intolerable as a complete juxtaposition to the din in the room. Think of it as party where someone takes the music off. Everything reverts to slow motions and a haze emerges before me of panic and confusion. Where do I go, how do I escape? There is no escape. We are thirteen floors up and no hiding place.

Everybody just stares.

'Police, stay where you are,' says I don't know who.

It doesn't matter if you were in on the job and had been on countless before. It still takes me aback.

The frenzy is over.

I am no longer standing holding the boy. He just stares at me. I am on the floor having taken a whack. Everyone is on the floor. I am staying in the role. But I am in pain – they are police not actors and they dish it out indiscriminately. Now is not the time to reveal my hand. I have to see it through. I have never met those storming the room before.

Suddenly the owner of the flat is pinned up against the wall. The boy is quickly removed as a female police officer ushers him to safety. His tormentors will never see him again. For now, his nightmare is over. It *is* all about the child.

To add to the chaos, the budgie is flying around.

They take the owner to the seedy filthy bedroom.

Computer disks are everywhere. The room is back in slow-mo. The individuals in the group recoil making no attempt to preserve or destroy the evidence but I must somehow come out of character and let it be known not to touch the computer.

One by one, the network is dismantled as each is led from the room. Someone picks me up. The officer definitely knows it *is* me. The other five officers seem very computer aware. They sense it is key evidence. My heart still races even though I know it is over. The group's faces paint a picture for the void that they portray. That excitement and control that they wore moments ago is now lost in their expressionless demeanour.

They are stunned. Time stops.

Edwin was trusted. Their checks were thorough. Nobody would come to a hellhole like this except them.

But now there is us.

My head is full – fear subsides and emotion rises. I have never known anything like it – my lifetime has been spent 'in the role' dealing with an undercover world but this is different. Today, I am feeling sensitivities. It is too early to know that I have a done good job – a fantastic job – I too am trapped in the moment, as stunned by my colleagues' entrance as my 'flatmates' were even though I knew, or believed I did, that it was coming.

I am exhausted but it will hit me later.

Finally, I am the last in the room. Time comes back to the present and the speed of everything around me approaches normal for the first time all afternoon. I don't look at any of them as they are taken away. Presumably later when they are questioned and thrown in a cell, they will conclude that I am not there. They will never hear from me again. There are no loose ends to tidy unlike Wales.

They can either naively decide that I was not charged and disassociated myself or that I was somehow in on it. I am sure they will all blame each other and through that they will notice my absence.

Alone in the flat, I can finally remind the officers that the computer is sacred.

'Don't touch that,' I advise. 'All the images are on there.'

They know to scoop up every single disk and check the fireplace for more. They scour the bedroom. If you hid one thing, you probably hid others.

As the moment calms, I do recognise one of the officers from a briefing. It relaxes me even though I already can feel I am amongst my own. It helps to begin the process of returning to normality – a friendly face even if it was one I didn't really know at all.

I am the only one to leave the flat not cuffed, but with a firm grip on my arm. The lift is working on the way down as I learn the truth for the delay.

My head spins knowing that soon I will be in a car taken away and a debrief will begin. I will never, thankfully, step in this building again. I am thinking these thoughts so I know already that 'this building' and 'this lift' – abstract language in the context of the whole – are demonising me when it is essentially the individuals, the images and the boy where the anguish will lie. I turn my back on all that is vile behind me. I won't come here again. Not a chance. I am calm but I know steam is flying off me.

As I cross to the police car that will take me to emotional safety, my colleagues take every last drop of evidence from the flat.

Except for one thing.

The greatest witness to all of this and all that went before is not seized and will not be called to testify.

The budgie lives to see another day.

23

'Fuck me, I can't believe you've just done all that.'

That was the greeting in the car.

'Can I have some *Lucozade*?' was the only response I could muster.

My sugar levels were low, my stomach was rumbling and in knots and my throat was dry but I hadn't realised it until now. That was the level of tension.

Now, having spent so long knowing that recall was my greatest strength and also a potential Achilles' heel, I go into immediate flashback. I am not saying much in the car but the mind is replaying.

I re-call the carer in my head and only now analyse my absolute determination to protect the boy at all costs, especially from that moment when I rang it in. These abusers were sexually driven and in their zone.

The voice in my head still keeps telling me – protect the computer too. I am living it all again moments after. I am trance-like. I am in the present and the immediate past. I am conditioned as an officer to do my job and leave others to do the same, to let events take their natural course. But I have slipped in the last couple of hours into being a human being and a parent so I am concerned about the boy but I do not have the energy, and nobody would know the answer if I ask of his whereabouts.

I assume he is safe. I know he will be. He is with the right authorities.

Save one child. All this – the training, Amsterdam, Wales – yes, it is worth it. The sterility of those early days and the understanding of the images, learning to react accordingly, even though it was some years ago now, were vital. They bear no relationship to the experience I have just had but I could not have got as far as I did if the drills hadn't taken me to the level it had and now, I suppose this creates a new bar for training because this is a real time experience. It was a reality not theoretical.

I realise it had been six hours in total. I had no idea. I had been so energised in not slipping up. It makes you wonder that when those rare occasions happen when you see a multiple day hostage siege on TV, how on earth people have the durability. I could have kept going but for the inevitability of nudity and participation. I was so far in the zone that I did not know it had been that long but now I realised, it became an exhausting statistic.

Everything I had done, I had for the role. All of it was against who I was as a person. Yet, I somehow found a way to be relaxed in character and parked that training. I can only explain it as building up a sub-conscious knowledge of likely scenarios and it sits there dormant as an overall picture but when the time comes, it is your skills that come to the fore. No training manual will give you a budgie and a lift that doesn't work. The most important lesson was that I had learned to see beyond the image. It didn't shock me because my vision went past it. That was the only way to get through.

Nobody ever says that they are an undercover cop. It comes with baggage. It normally suggests you have walked a moral plane and undertake work that is only slightly less scrupulous than those whom you are trying to nail. Colleagues are intrigued then take the piss. Look at us in Amsterdam. Perhaps now they see the worth.

I am sat in the police car. I do not realise I am soaking wet. I do not know when this sweat materialised. Nobody in the flat seemed to notice. Either I was doing my job well and it is only now that I am drenched or they were oblivious in their high state of giddiness. Perhaps it happened at the end as the stress literally poured off me. Everybody has their limit. Mine had just been tested to a new level.

Flashback: Soho with George. My bum is pinched. Why did I flinch? It is laughable in comparison. But I built up my 'job' hours, so to speak.

I had planned for today to happen in every capacity other than role-playing it through with the physical aspect, which we would never do. I had no idea it would end like this. I did not expect this reality. It is beyond my wildest dreams even though it will now become one of my most frequent nightmares.

I think of the legislation we were fighting. We have these guys absolutely hook line and sinker but I sit in the car thinking about the contamination of the computer. Have I done enough to preserve the scene? Have I been clear enough for the tape and has it picked it all up?

I tell myself these are issues for later. I have done all I can do for now.

The head is spinning.

I remember the owner of the flat implying that the boy will never make a disclosure. It plays on my mind. Surely now he has witnessed freedom and proper care too, and knows this is his moment to end this cycle and to speak out against it even at this young age.

The engine starts.

There is no conversation.

'Fucking hell, I can't believe you did that,' occasionally interrupts the glazed air in the car. I am not taking much in. I am being driven. That is all.

I barely even notice when we pull up at a hotel several miles away and I am met by the Head of Operations. I can no longer measure time *or* distance. I now have to relive it all in the debrief.

But it can wait.

I make for my room. I need to lose these clothes. Realities are kicking in.

'It's over, it's done.' I call home.

'How are things? How are you?' I am on auto-pilot, needing that contact but not taking it in. Home did not really know what *it* was. Julie just knew it was done, again, and I was on my way.

I am coming down, head still spinning. Going home is not actually an option. I am not fit to drive. I am shattered on the drugs of tension and adrenaline. But I feel absolutely fantastic. I know what I have done and I realise it is something that it has never been achieved in the history of the police. I know I have created new territory and that from here we must push on and our unit will be respected and we will not have to wait another two years for another opportunity.

I strip in the hotel room. I am wet and I feel filthy mentally and physically. I have never felt so unclean. The need to shower endlessly and scrub and re-scrub fills me. Nobody had touched me, though I had held the boy but the mental image of the *images*, and the ham sandwich, the bedroom and the budgie, the general dirt and the vile minds surrounding me make me disgusted with my own body and mind. De-guttering me is an impossible job. The physical starts now. The mental will be a task that never ends.

'I've done it,' I shouted, scrubbing harder.

'I can do it. I can do this.' I wanted to punch the shower curtain.

I needed to wash away everything in that room and of course, physically, that was possible. If there is an opposite of a breakdown where elation manifests itself through negativity and exhaustion then this is it.

We debrief. I replay what they don't know. They can see I am traumatised in delay but have meticulous and accurate recall. Still. I am told I have done well. All those months of mundane, that talk of chip shops and retail parks and my fake friend – it had come to this.

Even though there is no manual, everybody feels it is textbook. I learn only here that the lift hadn't worked and that the tail car had gone the wrong way at the flyover. It meets my budgie stories halfway as we laugh to relieve the tension.

A few drinks after filing my admin and I am gone. Out for the count I sleep and sleep and sleep. Then I have breakfast as though I have never eaten before. The previous day for now is a blur.

I drive home alone and I play it all back. I see Edwin next to me all the way. I pass the service stations where he set it all up. I feel the North looming as I hit the motorway. I have to rid it all from my system before I walk through the front door yet I have to park it too to be revisited because court is but a long way away. I speak to George and he is over the moon. Everybody had been vindicated. We knew this work was there. It just needed patience and investment in the right people. For me the drive back is an anti-climax. I just want home. That is what defines me even though I know I am being redefined by this experience.

Julie knows how to manage the family and is well aware of what I have been through but home life is important and my own experiences are put to one side almost immediately.

And I go to see Tom, the psychologist as soon as I can. I have a lot of bad dreams in the next couple of weeks. I spare him much of the detail. I tell very few people generally but in the undercover world of the police, most find out a few details. It becomes all Tom and I talk about in the next few sessions. This is the place to do it. My welfare and my family's are his only concerns.

I am having a lot of flashbacks, but at least with him, I could deal with them.

It is only later – much later – around 2004 and 2005 when I come to terms with all of this and often found myself getting emotional, reliving it and going back to the moment. Having been in that severe moment I have an affinity to how the victim of sexual abuse would feel.

But in the short time, it left me with no fear of what lay ahead in terms of work. Everything would be a piece of cake compared to this. From the worst place scenario, you could only rise and this was a hollow abyss.

A year later, The Midlands network were in court. The sentences were not great with none of them exceeding four years individually but 14 years in total for all of them. In 2017 they would have got double that. The judge said that they were a 'potentially dangerous ring that had been nipped in the bud'. The court were told that images of boys as young as five were of a sexual nature had been recovered. There had been no need for me to attend. I would have loved to go before them and look them in the eye to make sure that everything they did in the future they questioned. They had not seen me coming and would probably find another way to continue on release but for now they were crushed.

When I heard the news of their sentencing, I was just going about my business. I had moved on. Though, of course, you never could.

24

'Do you want a coffee, mate?' I was asked. 'You've been away a few months.' Had I really been gone that long?

'So what have you been doing?' There was always a bit of this.

'It's done now,' was all I replied.

I had gone back to work. Nobody *there* really knew what had gone on. There were whispers, of course. As much as I shut down that avenue of conversation back at my force so it was closed to me too. I was not about to fill them in on anything over-elaborate since it was not really in my nature and it seemed logical that this operation was just the beginning and more would follow so I would find myself back in this scenario again soon. I drew a line.

Equally I was not aware of what became of the boy. I still didn't even know his name. I learned only that he had been passed from pillar to post which explained the vacant immune look on his face – a tired tortured expression which did not complain as it might have done if it were the first time but which befell someone who had been here too many times.

I assumed he was being well looked after in care but there were no guarantees. In this kind of situation the cycle can repeat itself and it did not necessarily follow that he hadn't somehow slipped back into another similar scenario.

After the flat, no work was likely to seem the same again.

My senior officers back at Cleveland decided that my energies would be best focussed *not* in the undercover world but at Force Level where it was apparent that nothing was really being done. We were missing opportunities in seizing street buys and commodities.

So my task was to interview and select police officers for such roles and then train the officers in all elements of covert work but to a nationally recognised standard with all the elements of legislation, case law and practical and commodity knowledge.

I would get them young, which meant they were inexperienced and often naïve but had not been in the job long enough to be contaminated by police practices.

And we had instant successes. The drug dealers who were once barely pursued and if caught were never found to have the substances that justified our intelligence, were finally being banged up. We had to get up to date. It was now 1998. Cannabis was rife and heroin and crack were on the street, plus brothels and kerb crawlers. We made massive strides. The arrest and convictions of dealers, seizures of drugs and cash now regularly using video evidence clearly showed our intent. The work paid off. We took out every possible dealer in the force's remit.

Sentences became more regular and tougher. In all my thirteen years in the area, we only ever had one 'not guilty' and even that was overturned, sending the dealer to prison. These people knew no boundaries, one even stooping so low as to get his three year old to pass a wrap of heroin to an undercover officer. This was their level.

We were winning the war of minds getting national media coverage for clearing the streets and making communities safe. My young officers were duly recognised and suddenly in demand not just around the region but all over the country. The Middlesbrough Drug Unit, led by the late Inspector Mel Ashley, received two awards at the Association of Chief Police Officers National Drugs Conference in Belfast and Brighton respectively. We were now regularly penetrating organised crime gangs supplying Class A drugs and their complex networks.

In overseeing the safety, welfare and training of these officers, I felt I was giving my force something back and I know my judgement was trusted but deep down it was a pit stop. I knew that there was work to be done elsewhere and at the back of my mind one thought never left me. What happened in the flat was still going on elsewhere.

So, what next for me? I was keen to continue the work but equally the jobs had to come to me and to go straight to a similar mission might not have been the best option. I was only beginning to come to terms with what had happened and it would in time take me many months and years. I never went back to those retail parks, shopping malls and beaches where I had walked with Edwin so many times. I was not keen to revisit it and I did not want to see afresh how this magnet for young children in their innocence was a gift of an opportunity for predators knowing that security staff would be oblivious to any intentions of foul play. For the paedophile, it was common knowledge too that many kids who were missing from home would congregate in places like these. They were easy prey. As for the retail parks, I was never a great shopper but just endured them when I had to, waiting for my family but burying my head in a magazine in a coffee shop. I had seen too much and could spot signs the public would not notice. Yes, it made you very aware.

The undercover arena were keen to use what I had learnt on the operation as well and it became the mainstay of a course of many presentations which became the biggest part of my work until I retired.

This helped the mental side of dealing with it too and, as George had encouraged *me* in the beginning, I now did to others. I promoted myself as a specialist but I still had to be guarded because one flat job did not make a career and my mind was still with the hunger for live work and that may come at any time. You didn't want to compromise myself or over-egg your role in case you failed next time.

So, I began to promote the work of infiltrating the child sex offender with these presentations specifically about this operation running about four times a year to a class of around 25. The pool was small and in amongst them I hoped there would be at least another me or George. I remembered how George had always had that air of mystery about him where people had said he had been courageous but nobody really knew what he did. People were now looking at me through similar eyes. It was hugely rewarding to be involved for the vital work that needed to be done, for me unburdening the story a little bit more every time and for the feedback I received from those attending.

Much of this was disbelief that we actually went through with it. It was 1998. Everyone said it sounded horrendous. For me, they were conclusions for now. I did the job I was sent to do.

Many attending said they simply could not undertake this kind of work but had still learned from the courses – married with children was a major obstacle in recruitment even though I had overcome that hurdle.

The inability to talk openly about sex and the images was another stumbling block. In short, if you couldn't look directly at an image then you couldn't do the job.

Some of the traits of interception, of patience in a 'hostage' scenario, of recall and of creating openings into their world applied to many aspects of police work and that is what they would have taken from the courses but for many, it was a step too far to become me. Of course, I talked about many other aspects of policing but it always came back to the flat job.

I drilled too the need for Amsterdam and other similar countries where it might be advantageous, knowing that some places were really hardcore, and by 1999, one year on, the team went back out there for a repeat visit to top up our knowledge, more confident this time that we knew what were looking for and looking at. Once more we sat in The Blue Boy And Why Not, which Edwin had also visited.

Nothing had changed and that underlined one thing. The appetite was still there or indeed, greater. Surviving the flat job did not give me a divine right to be safe again. I had to be respectful of what I was up against. This time I took a lot more pictures. In time, having something like that on a phone would pave a much easier way to credibility than just saying you were there.

It cut straight through layers of bravado – imagery was the stepping stone of this language that these individuals understood. It had proved to be the key and moved things a long much quicker. The flat job exemplified that.

Imagine befriending an Edwin for months in a game of cat and mouse but evaluate too the simplicity that camera phones would in time bring to work like this in that you could leave one lying around for him to snoop on as he checked you out whilst you took a toilet break, and then he would know you were 'one of them'.

You would never have to put it on the table. Possession of photography would do the work for you. Once again though in Amsterdam, you still have to watch your own security and restrain your artwork to buildings and exterior shots. People themselves were a no go area because of who they could be with.

The world was getting smaller and anybody could be in those pictures and if it were your colleagues then you did not want to be justifying in the future who they were to a third party. So railway stations, canal boats and exteriors of sex shops plus football grounds, bridges and neon flashing signs but absolutely no individuals.

Even though Amsterdam had barely changed, only being there could confirm that. This is how I kept my momentum waiting for the next job – by training others and topping up my education. And there would be another job. I believed that totally.

The risk of the flat encouraged the Force rather than hindering ambition. It was a very difficult area of policing but it had to be done and the green light to re-visit the red light of the vice told me it was just a matter of time and that the unit was very much still live. They simply would not have sent us if there was to be no more work.

Nor was it through any lack of trying that meant the flat job stood as the solitary success to date. The intelligence was obviously much slower then and the resource to track individuals and networks pre-Internet was much less.

Across Europe too, this kind of work was very much in its infancy. Romania was a massive problem with many street children involved in under age sex acts there and even less legislation to prevent it.

I spoke there too through an interpreter – a trip most notable for casually wandering into town and ending up with 20 to 30 dogs in pursuit of me. I turned a corner to find a six-foot bear standing next to a four-foot six guy on a chain. The man, not the bear was enchained. It was not a bizarre sex act in the street. It was feral Bucharest. The group of us made an executive decision to head back to the hotel and didn't venture out again. Romania was barbaric at times – if this kind of stuff was happening in broad daylight, they had a long way to go before they could address the issues we were dealing with in the dark.

It was grim but also rewarding in that it underlined how we were leading the way, secondly to the United States of America and by 1999, British Police had launched *Operation Ore* which followed the Americans' *Operation Avalanche* where 100 people had been charged from 35,000 access records. Globally, it emerged that as part of this investigation, 390,000 individuals in 60 countries had accessed illegal material on the fledgling Internet. Much of this data came from one specific website. The information was passed to the British Authorities which by 2002 led to identifying over 7000 suspects, raids of 4000 homes and just short of 2000 arrests with most convicted. Around 140 children were removed from danger and as a result of what was then Britain's biggest criminal investigation into Child Pornography. Some 500 officers fell under the spotlight. There were also over 30 suicides believed to be as a result.

In this field there had never been anything close to this operation. This and the flat job became the two markers.

From a tactical point of view the two nations were leading the way. The legislation still fell well short of what was needed but *Operation Ore* and our unit gave enormous gravitas to the work. Essentially, we had been still working to legal parameters where sex with a twelve-year-old was the line in the sand and we were yet to know the dangers of online in full, even though *Ore* had begun to explode them. It was the dawn of the new century – some years before sites like Facebook emerged. The biggest challenges lay ahead for user, administrator and regulators like ourselves but we were just about at pace with it.

One case more than ever before the laws changed in 2003 underlined the fact that we were ready but the system was not.

And I was soon to get that phone call.

25

It is now July 2000. A little girl called Sarah Payne is missing in West Sussex near her grandparents' home after playing out with her two brothers. The nation is rocked by a very tough emotional case which in time would reveal many flaws in policing and underline how release from prison is never the end and the ability to re-offend, just like Edwin, is rarely too far away.

I was always waiting, forever ready. Despite the strain of the flat job, I was deflated that nothing similar had come my way since and it was clear very early on that the nature of this incident was vast and would be fantastic to work on, notwithstanding the grief for the family involved.

The parents Michael and Sara were quickly everywhere in the media appealing for witnesses but were soon told to prepare for the worst. Within 24 hours of Sarah's disappearance police had already visited several suspects including the flat of Roy Whiting who had been given a four-year sentence from 1995 for abduction and indecent assault. The maximum for this was life but he pleaded guilty early and received just the shortest of terms, even though one psychiatrist who analysed Whiting said that he was likely to re-offend. This verdict was to prove fatal for the Payne family. Indeed, he only served just under 2 ½ years and moved on his release to Littlehampton, also in West Sussex. He became one of the first individuals to sign the Sex Offenders Register but had refused to go on a Sex Offenders Rehabilitation Course.

By 10 July, police received an unconfirmed sighting at Knutsford Services on the M6 in Cheshire. By 17 July, a body was found in Pulborough just around 15 miles from where Sarah went missing. By the next day police confirmed it was her.

Whiting's initial questioning was *because* he was placed on the

Offenders' List. In terms of legislation, we were making progress. It did not mean, of course, that everyone who signed that would now be a suspect every time but in these early days after its inception, is undoubtedly significant in the trail leading to him.

When police called at his property he was not there, only to return some hours later when he was questioned for an hour.

After leaving, Whiting made for his car and was apprehended by undercover cops, held for two days, and then released with no supporting evidence against him.

On 20 July, a shoe belonging to Sarah Payne was found in a field. Whiting had a fuel receipt in his van from a garage not too far away despite his alibi that he had been at a funfair at the time.

But it was his own stupidity that did for him some three days later when he stole a vehicle and crashed it into a parked car after being pursued by police at speeds of 70 mph. He was charged with dangerous driving and remanded in custody until late September 2000 when he was sentenced to 22 months in prison.

This really was the key break in the case because it was going nowhere. It looked like a classic scenario of the police knowing but being unable to get a prosecution. The evidence had fallen kindly on Whiting even when his own carpet was analysed.

That was when I got the call from Scotland Yard to ask my availability. The answer would always be yes if my superiors cleared it.

'Do you think we have someone with the capability to infiltrate Roy Whiting?' Sussex Police had asked Scotland Yard. If they were coming for me at this stage in a case like this, it meant only one thing. They had probably exhausted all lines of enquiry or were keeping their options open.

I cancelled other work, just waiting, leaving colleagues frustrated. Ian was getting ready to disappear again for that thing he did that we don't know about.

I was told to be on standby in the July, but to be careful. They were pretty confident it was him but as ever, I now had to be doubly vigilant not to lead him down a path. I also had to step out of the media cycle. Obviously, I had seen the case but I began the process of switching it off and not asking for too much information so that I could slip into the role at a moment's notice – and this was different to what had gone before because we were following *possible* leads in the past. Now, we were playing catch-up and dealing with a live incident and somebody who could strike again.

These incidents *were* rare. Killing was a new level in abuse way beyond the sharing of images. I began to run possible scenarios in my head. I did not consider I was at risk, though a killer is a killer. His hunger was for children.

I had to work out how to get close to him knowing that his own security should be in overdrive. His fear level should have been at extreme. Interviewed so early after Sarah's disappearance, already on the list and then held for two days should have told him to keep his counsel small but I had to work on the basis that he might need to offload to one person and I had to back my communications skills that it would be me.

This time the talk would be different because I knew what he was and believed I knew what he had done. It was not a case of getting him to a scenario where all the cards might be put on the table in time like Wales or the flat. The plot was already written. I just had to hear it from him.

There was therefore, no need for innuendo or insinuation. This was all about building trust through small talk and hoping he had to unburden himself. I also did not know how long this would take. If I could infiltrate, it could be over in days or I may still be working him a year later. I knew though I had to be tighter than ever. No second chances. He had to slip at some point. The fuel receipt and the wrong alibi may have increased his own self-awareness but it told you one thing – that he wasn't actually that smart.

I tried to know little more than his name, which of course was not in the public domain at this point. I had to remove myself from the Paynes' grief because I knew that little Sarah was almost certainly dead when I got the call before her body was discovered. As a parent, I understood their heartache. If I was to be deployed, my emotions must stay idle. The professional had to kick in.

I spent the days waiting for the call, just trying to carry on with what I was doing. I had been here almost once before. A decade previously, Julie Dart had been kidnapped and murdered by Michael Sams in 1991. He had picked her up in the red-light district of Leeds, blindfolded her and placed her in a coffin-like box chained to his warehouse floor. After a failed escape, he smashed her head with a hammer. The following January, he abducted the estate agent Stephanie Slater after arranging to view one of her properties.

She too was held in a coffin for eight days, and after a ransom was paid, he fled and was only arrested after a reconstruction from the TV show *Crimewatch*. With many officers seconded from the Regional Crime Squad, we ran hours of surveillance painstakingly gathering evidence to assist in the investigation. I spent much of the time trying to track him and leaving leads of prostitutes' cards in phone boxes.

We couldn't know when he would strike next but we were pretty sure it was him. It was the public who really helped us convict him and in Sams and Whiting there were obvious similarities.

I was confident I could befriend Whiting. I knew I had those skills and I was certain he could crack because once you have committed a murder, you do not ever know what is around the corner. I didn't want to fail. I would get one window. The pressure and risk were huge and the police were out of leads after holding and releasing him. Two parallel issues hung over us. That clock was ticking again.

Firstly, media campaigns and the parents meant that the nation needed answers quickly. But secondly, the safety issue was paramount. Whiting, or whoever, was still out there.

Save one child. It's all about the child. But we hadn't. As that phrase came back to my mind, I knew that he could strike again. Sadly, Sarah Payne was gone but I had to save the next one.

I was set to go. There was never going to be the time that the other operations afforded me. On the return of the forensic results taken form Whiting's flat and van, I would head for Sussex. I tried to keep an open mind because as good that unit were, nobody could rely entirely on forensics. It was all part of a bigger picture. Plus – we were sure it was him so no cop could ever make the mistake of trying to make the evidence fit, however emotional the case was and whatever the level of public expectation.

But it was the stolen car that incriminated him – mistakes made under pressure after he had been drawn to the attention of the police.

I had been on standby for days when the call came to say I wouldn't be needed. This job would always bring hits and misses but of course, I was gutted. I was not stacking up career moments into a self-serving league table but given that this story had played out in public and that few knew of the flat job, it would have been even bigger than what happened in The Midlands.

I knew I was right for the job and could befriend him to bring this sorry story to its rightful conclusion and wanted that chance to underline the importance of the unit again but all that mattered was that the story ended as it did.

When Whiting began his prison term for dangerous driving, detectives carried out forensic tests on the vehicle. By the following February (2001) he was charged with the abduction and murder or Sarah Payne.

Pleading not guilty, he remained inside because he was still serving the previous time and by November 2001, a four-week trial began which would see key DNA evidence convict him. A member of the public had found Sarah's shoe, on which fibres from Whiting's van were found. It was the only item of her clothing that had been found. In this respect, Whiting had covered himself well. A strand of Sarah's blonde hair was also found in the van.

He was sentenced to life imprisonment and the judge said that life should mean life. His other crimes were then revealed to the public and a life of campaigning began for mother, Sara Payne and the notable campaign for Sarah's Law, echoing Megan's Law in the States where residents were aware of offenders on their doorstep.

As a parent, I believe you would want to know if these people were living in your street. As an officer you do not want vigilantism. That was the conundrum.

When these predators are released, like Edwin they go to a halfway house or similar. They have to prove they are not a threat. Many fail by breaching their conditions rather than re-offending itself. Look at Edwin, impatient to start all over again. Many never ever change. Indeed in 2001, I received word that some of The Midlands network were back together, though I have no concrete proof.

Through these tragic circumstances, there came only this positive. There was now momentum towards a change in the law and it would need to be far-reaching. The Roy Whitings of this world were soon finding new homes on the net. Sara Payne's work and the spotlight on the case definitely appeared to speed up the process.

It could not happen soon enough.

26

Early in the millennium, I had been promoted to Sergeant. I did not want to be desk or station-bound but it made sense to keep an eye on the career whilst the undercover stuff was running away with me.

There was a danger of me drifting into the system and not doing any more of this specialist work. There was a very strong possibility I might return to uniform. At my time of service, I did not really want this. I respected that work but my heart and hunger lay elsewhere.

As one manager put it to me: 'You get promoted and you look despondent'. It was just not necessarily where I wanted to be. By 2002, Police Forces in general were starting to really invest in online. It was possible our days as a specialist were numbered.

Needless to say, my wife Julie was over the moon. She had encouraged me to apply. Taking exams had almost become an annual event. My father would been ecstatic too at the path my career had taken since urging me to leave Cornwall. I had always paid lip service to it as a concept.

I did the work and it took me where it took me.

But what this now meant was that if I was asked to do the specialist work, an approach would have to be made for me and they would have to sign it off.

In 2002, that call did come and I was away again on secondment from February to October but my then Chief Constable had assured the unit that they could have me for as long as it took. I then got the news that my promotion to Sergeant would stand and that any such posting would be looked upon my return.

This again showed much support for which I was very grateful.

And that is when I wandered into Malcolm's life.

He had served eight out of a twelve-year sentence. His release had imposed a four hour only release window.

Its only advantage seemed to be to lose that stigma that I was always off on a jolly yet the few who worked with me closely would have known that it would kill me. I did not want that career. I had created my own luck and always thought that if you did a good job, it would enhance your credentials and that journey meant that I craved undercover work for the challenges and the results – the chance to change people's lives. For that reason only, I owe Malcolm a small debt of thanks, in a twisted kind of way. I draw the line at that.

I had to try to get to meet him. That window was small – more narrow than Edwin's. The chance to infiltrate was less than it had ever been. But I knew I could do it.

This meant more preparation work than I was used to – greater than any before – but it became clear from the intel that he frequented a small café near a market and that not many people were ever inside so that would be the ideal location and I would make for there during his four hours out.

He was an odious man – horrible to the point that your hair would stand up on end, permanently self-centred with a massive ego, rock solid in his confidence in speaking to other women. He thought he was God's gift and was only interested in sex. I knew anything over the age of seven was too old which was extremely distressing as we were now talking about children of the same age as my own. He was on a par with Roy Whiting. I would need new skills to keep pace with Malcolm. His self-belief was like nobody I had encountered so far with the possible exception of Mr Big from Thailand.

I learned too that all his offending had been committed on his own. That made things slightly difficult in that I knew that he was the job in its entirety. He wasn't going to lead me to a bigger picture and there was nobody in a network whom I could play against him. He was a loner, and that was it.

Crucially, he was obsessed by phones – this was his bit of ego knowledge to play to. Again, they all like to think that they are experts. For the purposes of the job, I got an identical mobile.

Just as before we had a few dummy runs, trying to pick the best place and opportunity, dependant on the pre-work establishing his movements. But now it was time. Another windy day and I am sat in a vehicle in a multi storey car park, pondering my move.

Malcolm is oblivious to the watchful eyes and is strutting around the markets.

I am ready to go, but like many times before I am anxious, hoping that he is heading as normal towards possibly the one place he seems to find comfort in. The Café. It is small and cramped with a few tables and long bar area. Not much room, but in a strange way ideal for my purpose – tight like the restaurant in Wales.

The call comes up that he has entered and so, the technical is on and I am out of the vehicle. I go from waiting, to in the zone in seconds, now walking with a purpose towards the cafe not knowing what to expect. Is he alone, meeting someone, or getting a take out? My mind is focussed and I am now committing myself but will have to decide on the spur of the moment how to instigate some communication.

The pressure is building I take the stairs down from the multi-storey car park and get ever closer to the location. I have one chance. Again. As normal. Your first chance to make a good impression can also be the last chance saloon. The pressure intensifies.

I enter the café. Now, it is nearly full with Malcolm sitting alone with a table, and facing towards the counter. I walk up towards him.

I pretend to look around for somewhere to sit whilst scanning the menu. We almost have no choice but to sit together.

'Can you keep a eye on that mate please?' I ask casually, placing my mobile and carrier bag on the table and turning towards the counter.

He looks up at me. The first eye contact.

'No problem,' he replies.

I order a cup of tea and a cake and pause as I wait for my order. I glance back in his direction. Perfect. He is looking at his phone but also glancing towards mine. I am in.

I sit down with my drink and cake next to him.

'Cheers for that,' I offer.

'No problem,' he replies.

'I have this phone, it's new but it's doing my head.' I throw it out there too see if he engages.

'I have the same one,' he responds.

Spot on. But of course, I know this.

'Don't get me wrong, it's small but the controls and putting my contacts on are a nightmare…let alone understanding the set ups. They are really testing me.' I was calling for an expert again.

'I'll show you… nothing to it really.'

And so it began.

Malcolm started to talk me through the phone, the controls and processes of how it worked. The expert was in his element and in control showing his knowledge, only casually interrupted by my enthusiastic appreciation. He revels in the role showing his expertise with more than I asked for taking my handwritten numbers from my paper and entering them for me.

One hour in and I am ordering more tea. The ice is well and truly broken. He exudes confidence. Arrogance, perhaps. I remain subservient, knowing my place. I allow him to show his authority.

Before we leave, he places his number in my phone and I reciprocate. I have allowed him to take control, Now and again, I have butted in with general chat, purposely slowing it down allowing us to bond.

I try to keep the contact going. He needs to look around the market and suggests I tag along if I want. I do not need a second invitation.

It is market day. He can blend in. So can I. He takes me from one massive indoor venue to another outside, loving looking at his cheap bargains. I buy some dusters to appear engaged. I needed to lay down my cover story to make that next meeting happen. Within minutes he knows that I was looking for long term opportunities in the area. The seed is sewn…

I told him that I was a sports coach and that I teach kids indoor activities. That should be enough to whet his appetite. But I also threw in that I had a car. He already had everything he needed from me in moments – meal ticket and children.

I had dangled some carrots and he was hooked, so I suggested that we should meet up again playing on the fact that I was still new to the area.

He had found a friend. We agreed to meet a second time. No surprise – at his suggestion that would be at the start of his release time from the hostel. I knew that but did not draw attention as we parted company at the end of the market without a second glance, confident I could do the rest with his phone number in my phone.

Once again, the research was key and firm proof that detail as trivial as a mobile phone can break the ice and enable you to make an approach.

This job finds me in a market town on the East coast of England and the year is 2002.

I was under a new operational team and Investigating Officer who had not been here before with me and each of them were amazed that two strangers would just click. At this level in my experience, I would have been disappointed with anything less.

Malcolm had told me little and I only absorbed the information to tick it off against what I knew, to establish if he generally told the truth or not, so I learned that he lived in the vicinity and little more. But I knew he was at the hostel. He hadn't technically lied though.

It was clear early on that this dynamic was different. He had no interest in me. There was no hands on knees scenario like Edwin. I was his driver and I began the weekly routine of going to retail shopping centres, market stalls and malls. These were classic magnets. I made out that I rarely shopped but would love to explore these big complexes on the edge of town.

'I have never been. I have heard it's a bit of a shopping centre,' I played naivety the first time he invited me there.

He told me it was massive but I knew why we were there and of course, it was always busy. Perfect for him. When you look back on it, why would two grown men walk around a place like this not really buying anything?

He was looking. His eyes were cast. He was on the prowl.

He had taken my lead and led me into many sports shops so I could find my own level and the conversation could revert back to the story I had told him. Though, not initially. He was working me from a long way out too, and it figured that if we were looking at equipment and clothing, he could slip a line here or there about what my 'students' might be using or wearing as he got to know me a little more. Retail parks of the North were not a one off for the predator. A pattern was emerging that they flocked there. And Malcolm was impatient. He just wanted young girls.

We became more and more comfortable with each other without disclosing anything. It was the usual pre-game cat and mouse, building trust and escalating to something, but he was unsubtle yet sly, continually eyeing people up. But one day when I picked him up, he seemed to unburden:

'I did have a cloud,' he confessed. 'I had a few problems.'

'That sounds interesting,' I lied, knowing exactly what they were.

'I assaulted someone protecting a woman,' he confessed. 'The man was violent and picking on my friend but I ended up in prison.'

'How bad is that?' I feigned injustice knowing that his explanation of prison was not the truth.

'I have had some problems too but I did not go to prison,' I interrupted him in full flow.

His guard was down. It was a good moment to fake empathy. Clearly, this offloading outburst was pre-determined. He had been weighing up his trust for me and felt that now was the time. It was obvious to see because it began as soon as he got in the car.

'The police did not really want to know and did nothing about my flat being set on fire,' he continued.

The sense of being harshly treated was normal in these people.

'It's a bit of a long story,' he assured me which was his way of saying that he had done wrong but we would leave it there. He was trying to create a new trust by showing that his past could be considered unblemished. If he put something out there, I would have no questions and he could continue unchallenged. It was a clever technique to offer it out but then dismiss it. He did not know I was a cop obviously but it lulled you into believing everything he said to be true. Unless you knew otherwise. He didn't need to put it out there and had done so only partially. It was also an invitation to me.

'The girl next door tried to do me for indecent assault,' he continued.

He really was sticking to the truth – except in his tone. By suggesting that she had only *tried,* he was clearly implying that she had failed. It had all been a terrible misunderstanding.

A similar thing had happened to me, I reminded him again.

'That's why I am here, a fresh start,' I alluded.

I, too, was looking for a chance of a new start. But he was only half-listening. I had already passed the trust test and he felt comfortable. Sharing the same just opened him up more without him pursuing me over my own exploits to the degree that he even named the officer involved in his case and the fact he had nothing but hatred for the officer, which was dynamite really because I could feed it back and check how much of what he was telling me was close to the truth. I hadn't even needed to lead him here. For one so confident, he wound himself up into this state. It had clearly been brewing for a long time.

I knew he had been arrested in the past and the details of the victims and their ages. He continued to lay the blame at the police's door. It rang true of that 'we love children' mentality and the 'police colluded with the media to create words like grooming and paedophile' stance. There was almost without exception any example of these people admitting guilt.

Somebody else had always upset the apple cart.

'When I know you a little better, I'll tell you my own story,' I pretended to share the experience to continue letting him open up.

But for now, I took great heart in the fact that he was telling me mostly the truth. I had become closer to him than in the first two meetings than Edwin on the flat job. I deduce that is for two reasons – Edwin made a move on me *and* he was not a lone operator. I rejected him but he was always one of a network. Malcolm *was* alone and had no desires on me. He only saw me as a companion and a driver. I had declared my hand in being of similar tastes. He had nothing to lose in opening up – in his mind.

I was tuned into him. I could always tell without even observing him that he was looking around. Everything and everyone young was an opportunity from areas where music played to food outlets to play areas to TV shops. He did not go to retail parks to buy things. He only wanted to steal and the subject of his theft was someone else's innocence.

We *were* getting on well and although I observed him stalking young girls in a sly manner cowering his head down and then raising his eyes to survey them, he had kept his own thoughts to himself initially before this outpouring. But I clocked them.

Then from nowhere one week, he suddenly suggested we go further afield.

'Let's go to the city' he said.

This, I felt, was unlikely but I could see that it was a major positive. I was trusted. He felt he could risk his parole hours to go further afield and I could break him a little more in the car journey. My head was thinking of Edwin. He had used me to get further afield. Now, Malcolm was doing the same. It was becoming standard fare for the recently released. At some point their lack of self-control coupled with the predator within meant that they simply had to travel out of their region.

He also wanted to tell me something else. I was now his only confidant.

'I've met someone online,' he began. 'I think I've fallen in love.

It transpired that he had only met her the day before, and of course never actually *met* her and this would happen time and time again. He, more than anyone, would keep our Ops Team busy. Every time he had a new love, they would have to check it out and risk assess. I needed to remind him of what I did.

'I do lots of one to one coaching,' I fuelled him up.

'I'd love to see you coach,' he lied, meaning of course that he would love to see whom I coach.

'I think I know who you are,' he kept saying.

But by now, we had only met three or four times. This was slow work compared to his standards with women but he was checking me out for other reasons. I believe he took a lot from me not pursuing him over his story of how he ended up in prison. He had told me the underage assault accusation. I think he read between the lines from me saying no more than I had experienced something similar. Sometimes the unsaid gave as many clues as the words you did speak.

What he really was trying to tell me was that he thought I had a similar interest to him, even though I had not even got anywhere near that. I had let his imagination run away with him.

'Well, you don't really know me,' I reminded him.

That was the benefit of the wire so we could clearly trace back that I had not goaded him in this direction.

'Well, look, what *do* you like?' The car journey had given him the security to open up. That he was even in the car at all suggested I was in a small circle of trust that consisted of just one.

I took him back to the girl.

'Yeah, I did have a problem,' he confessed. 'You don't just come out with it, do you?'

And he was right. This is why we worked people slowly over a long period of time. They give you a little, then a bit more. On the second time it comes up, they have already overcome that hurdle of putting it on the table, so they can edge forward a bit more knowing that you did not react adversely the first time. That is why it is cat and mouse and it is built slowly.

'You can trust me,' I lied.

'It was all a misunderstanding,' he maintained, as I would expect – forever in denial.

'I was given an introduction to a girl...she fell in love with me...it was not full on...she was testing the water...'

'That sounds nice,' I interrupted.

He had flagged up after our third chat that he had done time but had added little more than he had assaulted someone, sparing the details of anything sexual or with a minor. It had burdened him, for sure, but only to test me to see if I reacted.

He always continued as if there was nothing wrong:

'I'm just biding my time,' he would say. 'Then, I am going to get my own place.'

He was never going to say that he was a sex offender. He couldn't know me well enough to know if I would attack him as many feel they should when greeted with such conversation but equally this was not the paedophile's type of language. He felt he had done nothing wrong and that would never change.

I enjoyed the journey. But only really for the breakthrough I was making. Not going to retail park complexes was good. It broke the routine and that was beneficial for both of us. It meant new conversation and different reactions to extract from him from a different environment. There was nothing forced, though. We got on well. Our relationship became better with this disclosure.

'Look at that school there,' he blurted out as I tried to find somewhere to park.

It was the fish and chip shop part two. I drove right up to the gates. And then he told me more of what he had done historically. I didn't flinch but I was glad that it was totally accurate. Not only did he feel comfortable doing so but he wasn't lying. I had him where I wanted him. Untruths were hard to keep up with and there was always likely to be a curve ball but it was much easier to spot if the subject had been consistent in everything else.

I am sure there is nothing spontaneous in the way he blurted it out, leaving me little option but to go along with it. It was a test but it represented that our relationship was getting somewhere. To coincide with this after a period of time, his freedom had been extended. For example, he was allowed unsupervised visits to his parents for his first time whereas even to them there had been restrictions because they had children and minors in their street. He was being given the message that society was welcoming him back.

More tests. With each conversation, he would add more and more. The real Malcolm was emerging at every turn.

I pull up at a pre-determined car park. We had parked there a few times over the months with a solitary guy on watch in a portacabin. We leave the car just near the railway station and walked through towards the indoor markets – always the same type of venue. He told me he had to go there to get his bearings.

We are in the zone having a good look at various stalls indoor and out. Occasionally he comments on young girls that would pass our way. We pause for refreshments and he is watching the clock because of his release conditions so our stay is brief and it is back to the car – I am testing him as is he me. I am focussed as normal. There is a new scenario at the car park.

Operations and situations can change and when they do you have to weigh up options and then try to recover. Sometimes you have to walk away. You have to think like a criminal.

The test came from an unlikely source.

'Someone's been at your car,' the attendant rushed to tell me.

'You what?' I asked knowing that Malcolm was in earshot and I couldn't deny the comment.

Nobody needed the public jeopardising a routine op where there was nothing to show. You cannot blame him. Not everybody on car park security was that vigilant. Now, Malcolm is in a different mood. One minute his eyes are on female girls, now surveillance is up. His liberty is at stake.

'Have a look at your boot,' the attendant urged. 'Two men were having a pop at it.'

Then it registered. I knew exactly what he was saying.

The lads were looking out for me. We had a pretty standard routine op that if I was gone for a certain period of time then the backup would make the decision to check technical equipment.

'Are we being followed?' he goes into overdrive. 'I want to check the car.'

These things happen near city centres. People do try boots and door locks but it unleashed a layer in him, which I had not seen amongst all his bravado or confessing persona. Suddenly, he doesn't know who I am again for a while. It is as though I do not exist and now he is getting paranoid. I have to try to avert it and calm him down. Easier said than done. He is having none of it.

'Come with me while I check the car,' I try to becalm him. 'Look, it's locked. It's not unlocked.'

He returns to the passenger seat while I visit see the security guy once more. He cannot see what I am saying to him so it makes it easy for me to return and blame him.

'He's not quite right,' I shake my head in fake disbelief. 'He's all over the place. He's on some sort of gear.'

I hope that would be the end of it but Malcolm begins to pull down the glove boxes and flip the visas. I need to rein this in and get driving to pacify him to show there is nobody following us. I knew they had just checked the vehicle.

The kit was much now more sophisticated than what I had even in the flat job. They couldn't know if we would walk back across the forecourt when they were swapping but they had to take that risk. I couldn't have *him* looking for everything. I have to hit the road.

We talk a lot – him in his agitated state and me reminding him that the security guy was not all there and couldn't really see from his sheltered cabin. Also, it has delayed us, forcing Malcolm to ring ahead to say that we would be late, which was always the first level of security activation and would embarrass him when we both knew that on other occasions he would be genuinely running over because he had been up to something. He wanted to play that card as infrequently as possible. This time it was not his fault.

'Look, I am going to take some detours,' I tell him. 'I want you to look in the mirror to see if we have any strange cars with us.'

This perhaps was a clue to the policeman in me but he was so restless he would not have noticed.

I know on this occasion that we are not going to be followed. I can be as elaborate as I want. Bringing Malcolm in to assist me on watch should re-assure him and strengthen our bond when he reflects. I spend fifteen minutes doing manoeuvres. This is known as anti-surveillance. He begins to calm down but remains wary for the remainder of the journey.

This is proof of how things can change and indeed suspects with them. Self-preservation is all that counts. Re-assurance that you are not under surveillance come a close second.

By the time we arrived near his hostel, it had actually enhanced my credibility because it looked like we were *both* being targeted and had got away with something as partners in crime. To survive a scare gave us a deeper connection in his eyes. He never saw me as part of it, he regarded me as having escaped it with him as we were both as bad as each other, even though I hadn't revealed any specifics of my hand. He had seen and heard enough from me that he believed I was him take two. He just didn't know the details.

And when we returned a second time to the same city everything passed without incident. I felt we went up a notch again and between February and August this was the pattern. Back and forth to retail parks and visits to nearby cities. He certainly had an eye on something there and from now on I would be the one to deal with any technical issues.

But he was behaving himself and everything seemed in order except that the intelligence was telling us that he was using the equivalents of the social media of the day such as chat room and his mobile to trap single mothers. This was something we were very wary of because all the standard traits of somebody like a Malcolm suggested that he would gain the trust of the mother leaving her undoubting of his reliability and warmth so that he could then work the children.

He was becoming more and more acquainted with females he had met online. Of course, all the women had children. For that reason when I was not with him I had to have my dirty phone with me in the off chance that he may call.

My alarm bells were already ringing when he called me as I was out with my family at a retail park ourselves. Furthermore, it was one of those rare occasions when I could be compromised. The ambience and background noise of a shopping centre could be explained by anything or anyone but instantly I had to walk away from the family to take the call.

There were still moments like this when the two worlds merged.
  'I've got a surprise for you, he began.'

27

Knowledge and hindsight now flagged this key word up to mean anything other than that. The word 'surprise' meant that the individual was pursuing their own agenda. They were up to something. And I would be part of it.

'We're gonna do some painting.' He beamed.

'Oh right,' I replied. 'How long for?'

'A couple of days, if that,' he informed me. 'I have met someone online and she is separated with two children and I love her,' he stated.

He seemed to have it all worked out – a plan that I would say was his standard. I knew why he was taking me – transport. I was also another set of eyes for him and he did trust me but essentially, I was his A to B vehicle. I knew that he had only ever offended on his own before. He was using me but he may have to discard me too.

'Pick me up at 11 a.m.' He resonated confidence.

The old Malcolm was back.

Meanwhile I had to ditch my family and speak urgently to the Operational Heads as this was a potential situation. He was controlling the timeline.

So a couple of days later, the two of us met up, not before I had spent hours discussing scenarios over child safety. I knew little except that Malcolm had told me that 'she' was in her 30s and had been through a rough time.

'We'll do the labour, you get the materials,' he had promised.

The parent was hooked. He had preyed on her vulnerability and exploited it.

Travelling to the house, our operational teams are on standby. Of course I am trying to be curious about the woman, asking as a mate would how they had met. I know the answer. Social networking struck again.

Malcolm's usual slimy patter hooked the parent unwittingly. Again, he would groom them for the process of then going for the children.

The kids were under nine so it fitted his offending profile. What we don't know is *their* movements. Essentially, are they in the house?

On his directions we travel to a housing estate on the South coast. I am on high alert. There are echoes of the flat job in my head. I park up outside the house while Malcolm grooms his hair, brushing it back with his hands. Slimy in every sense.

The lady has no idea who I am and she really knows less about him even though he had begun to gain her trust. He had agreed to work for nothing if she found the money for the bits and bobs for the house. You can trace it back without any case knowledge to spot a vulnerable single mum bemoaning that she had no time or skills to decorate her place with two young kids and he spotting the Achilles' Heel and pounced. Just like we sought out that expertise that many paedophiles seemed to have in a niche field and played it as a way in, his own method was similar. He waited for her to push a button and then made his move. Our techniques were the same. We were just on different sides of the law.

Nothing exposed that more than when we enter the house.

He knocks firmly and on first impressions does not seem vulnerable, quite relaxed and happy to let us in. In fact, naively she announces she is off to town with a friend so gives us the run of the place, adding that she would be gone for a couple of hours.

She asks if we want some fish and chips bringing back. I smile to myself that the British chippy has no idea how important its role is in my work! I only see her again later at the dinner table when she returns with the food and I have no option at that point but to play it straight down the line.

There was no obvious tension or *sexual* tension between them. She had no idea how he had behaved in her house nor that it was not her he wanted:

She had opened her house to strangers whom she barely knew. It was the first time she had seen Malcolm. She gave us the house alone unsupervised. Thankfully the children were at school.

While she was out we had begun painting.

The wallpaper comes out. I make for the garden to tidy that up. It is the most unusual role-playing in an undercover role so far. I am now doing some gardening and decorating for a living.

But it is a double-edged distraction. He is keen to show her he is a good guy who would do anything for her. Also, he wants to inspect the house, making his way from room to room, opening the drawers and looking at the children's clothes. He pays particular attention to the under garments examining them in detail.

His language turns to graphic:

'I am gonna do the children, and I am gonna do the mother,' he announces totally confiding in me but without any element of concealment.

He just blurts it out.

He loves the power and the knowledge that he is already controlling and when she returns, he gives her an almost 'sorry to let you down throwaway' by suggesting it is going to take longer than he thought. He sees it as a great opportunity. He is buying his return just like I always tried to ensure a second get together but there is no warmth on their parting – no kiss goodbye. I just shake hands with her. We must have been there only three hours. It would all have appeared normal. Ensure the next meet. That was all that mattered to both of us for different reasons. Though, I did tell him I would not be able to make it more than once a week because of my other commitments. I needed to work him a little too.

The car journey home was appalling. He spent the whole time telling me he was going to break them all and have sex with each of them. He spent most of his time on his phone before looking up to tell me. In between he announced that he had sexually abused a child at a holiday centre. This state of frenzy that the house visit had given him placed us on high alert. He was on maximum disclosure to me again and we had a duty to do the same.

He pushed me on my coaching and I knew he was reading for bursting. I told him of this young girl I was working with one to one and his giddiness-cum-aggression went to a new level but I had to pull it back because I could not be seen again to take the lead and fall later into Agent Provocateur, which under English Law is seen as exclusion of unfair evidence with entrapment.

This is so important because if you are not patient and fall into the trap of rushing then this could finish your case, with a judge hounded by the defence.

I began the process of dropping the girl in over the next few months but did so whilst he was at his most uncontrolled. He didn't even ask for a photo. Such was his disgusting controlling predatory nature that there was no concept of 'physical beauty' – age and access were more important.

The questions were coming at me thick and fast but at the back of my mind there was still one problem – under the current legislation I was still only likely to get him charged as being a nuisance under common law. We were struggling for offences.

He was worming his way in and we had to stop it before he might attempt a lone visit back to the house. We never saw the children in person but I knew from the pictures and the language that he was serious and meant what he said and he would tell her loved her after just a couple of days to get to where he wanted to be, re-assuring her that she didn't deserve what had happened to her in the past but she did warrant better, and that was obviously him.

This was his grooming technique, taking the mother to an extreme position rather than the child, and opening her up on her troubles so she would collapse like a pack of cards in her gratitude.

We knew he was doing this to more than one woman at a time, hiding and lurking in forums from behind his phone. We couldn't know what we hadn't been able to stop so far.

I had no hesitation in passing everything from the house to my bosses but we still wanted to keep him live. They had no choice but to make certain disclosures which meant the lady in question would learn just how close she had been and probably would set her own trust back several months if not years. A historical case of one girl at the holiday camp that he confessed was also addressed but she had managed to find some closure and did not wish to proceed as a witness.

On this occasion, we had been able to prevent two innocent children *before* damage was done. I *had* to call it in – so explicit was he in his language that he would move to the next stage at the first possible opportunity.

Whether I could keep him live outside of this, it remained to be seen. So when we met the next time, I asked him straight how all that was going and when we were likely to be going back painting.

'She doesn't want it anymore,' he confessed but with an air which told me that he didn't really care and would soon be moving on to the next target but crucially did not associate me with the rejection.

I was still his driver, his alibi, his meal ticket. In many ways this is the perfect result because we prevented him, without children being risked at all and we still had him so we could effect the same result again.

But he was clearly ready to swoop and very hungry to do so. It is possible that I may have been frustrating him and made him worse. We were a little one step forward and two back but we stuck together and his language showed no sign of abating. We went to the seaside for the day, and on the beach, he was constantly watching children playing, particularly one girl between six and eight riding a donkey.

'I'd like to jump up and down on her,' he made no shame of telling me.

I doubt he knew the legislation inside out at this point but I was aware it was firmly on his side. I was an officer of the law, witnessing this language and intent but with no further powers unless I stuck with him and it took me closer.

So, I joined him on visits to his parents, who stood by him seemingly unconditionally. They didn't know he rarely mentioned them when he was not there. Even they were a means to an end. He asked me if I would like to see his bedroom. Of course, I had to go along with it. There stood a picture on the side of a relative. He confirmed the worst:

'I am gonna do her when she's the right age.'

I had never witnessed this level of aggression previously. This was not for my benefit. This was how he was. In the arrest at the low-cost hotel, I felt just like I was busting someone naïve with needs. In Wales there was a lot of posturing and secrecy. At the flat, I had broken down that wall over months. Here we had a loose cannon, hell-bent on aggression, control and abuse with no level of discretion and his parents, through duty, stuck by him.

Yet, he was grooming me as well. At the back of this mind was this silent undercurrent that I was a sports coach with access. He would continue on his own mobile phone luring but he always knew that he could play me too. He was working me to get to my non-existent pupils as he had done the decorating to get to the lady's children.

Amongst all this, whilst we monitored him and his phone as much as we could, his movements were still very limited yet we could not know everything. There was another life that we were not party to.

I was due to meet Malcolm next outside his hostel and assumed we would be gone for the allotted four hours. He emerged bandaged around the face, blaming a gardening accident at his parents when a spade had bounced up and hit him in the face. It didn't ring true. I couldn't help but wonder if something from the past had come back to haunt him. He had so little opportunity to get into such a scrape that it all looked very suspicious. I had not encountered this kind of scenario before.

I couldn't get sucked in. Instinct *kicked* in. Much of my role was still focussed on the recall. Now, I had to think ahead to court. We had so much on him and all the signs were that he was going go to offend but we could not pursue this man for eight months only for the defence to levy against us that we had abused the fact that he might be on tablets and he was not therefore firing on all cylinders with this injury. I had to visualise court 18 months from now and with the still very vague legislation, I had to wait it out and see the bigger picture. You had to make decisions that were right for you, the person and the case.

On this particular occasion we had people watching us so I took one look at him and made that call. He looked dreadful, was carrying tablets and clearly not himself. Any confession on that day would be worthless. His defence would be that he was on medication and play heavily on his injuries.

Everyone watching thought the operation had been compromised when they saw me turn the car around and parked up outside the hostel. Only in the debrief did they realise that I had aborted. You have to be considered but also split-second. Knowledge of your suspect and the likely techniques of a legal time some months down the line are a lot to deal with in the moment.

It was not an isolated moment. Not long after, we were out when one of the original golden rules came back into play. Do not put yourself in a position where the unknown can throw everything into chaos.

We were returning from the market when suddenly we had to make a detour. We spotted a crowd coming towards us and I spied fear in the girl's face heading our way.

I knew what was going on before he told me that we had to get out of there immediately. He just ran for the car.

'I recognised someone over there.'

But I was ahead of him.

'I did her when I was young,' he confessed once more.

Was this the truth behind the gardening accident?

The macho bravado with which he swaggered around both his own parents' and complete strangers' houses had suddenly seen his own reflection in the mirror and couldn't deal with it. For a brief second the bully turned coward and he got a whiff of the fear that abuse bestows on its victims as he anticipated a baying mob pursuing *him* if the girl in question were to wail even the slightest acknowledgment.

Being trapped in her own mind or that embarrassment that abuse sometimes to those who have suffered, perhaps made her double-take and rendered her mute but I saw the look on her face and the same fear was mutual. He panicked.

As perverse as it sounds, I only had a duty of care for Malcolm's safety. That is the brief. The force could not risk a counter claim in the same way that I couldn't expose a paedophile if they were on medication with a bandaged head because their make-believe gardening had injured them. The crime would always be ours not theirs.

I later understood that this was part of what he had been sentenced for in the past. It is possibly the only time that I have seen that realisation amongst those whom I had infiltrated. I look back and in itself see it as a rare moral victory but in the moment, I knew that it would not last.

It was a brief wake-up call on a par with the 'tampering' of the car in the city but it would not deter him because his whole make-up was predatory and his sexual instinct was abuse. It only scared him at the time to see the girl now older and more mature, enjoying herself with friends *and* she was no longer in his age bracket for him to find her his type any more.

It was a different proposition and she appeared as though she had survived him bar that one haunted look she threw his way. It was he who recoiled but they both knew. She was fighting back with her life but seeing him took her back. He was defeated because she was now a young woman and he didn't have that control. He shrunk into his seat – a rare realisation of what his evil meant to a victim. I cannot say for sure but I am pretty confident that it was the only time in my presence that a victim had set eyes on their abuser years down the line.

Something was about to give – either in him and his ability to crack, or his desire for the next victim. He was still on to me about my coaching.

Equally, every time we spoke, he was killing me with all the latest women he was lining up with no real desires for them other than as an access point to their children. He was even talking to women in mainland Europe and Australia which was daft really because he had no hope of a rendezvous given his parole – unless his self-belief convinced him that they would come to him, which was entirely possible with his mindset. Every new attempt at a conquest brought no new trepidation for him. He genuinely believed he was God's gift to women, which told you everything about the mind. He had no real sexual desires on them but he knew he could work his magic. So, it was never a physical challenge towards the adult but it was mental – all about control. There is an argument that some paedophiles are born that way and so it can't be helped but he knew exactly what he was doing. He had a full set of capacity, so this was abusive in that he was deliberate and his method was to own the victims' mind.

From the language he used describing frequently how he would 'do' both adult and child, he did not seem to fall into that category where his sick desires were something you might understand. He had no line, no borders – sex was control, aggression and power. And I remained no different in his game – because he was comfortable with me, I was being used to the maximum as a confidant to being his chauffeur.

The only time his self-belief was knocked and he questioned his powers was that near-encounter with a former victim. When you see the mask drop like that, you really can strip back the layers with ease of the lack of substance and messed-up head of the individual.

I knew we were coming to a conclusion. Of course, I had to call in the previous incident and that placed us in an even more 'aware' situation. As with the painting and decorating job, disclosures were being made almost every time now he gave me new intelligence, more so than in any other case.

I ramped up the fictional girl I was coaching and the mystery worked him into a further state. To underline the point that control came before sex, he never asked for a photo. There can be few cases in attraction when you do not need a picture, surely. Yet, I was never allowing myself to feel the pressure of delivering this young girl to him. I knew every time I could wait it out because he would run out of probation hours.

That also showed the other side of the problem from our point of view. I could not realistically supply. I could not lead. That would blow the case out of the water. I was getting a sense that the legislation again meant that this had come as far as it could once more.

But we had him out of his comfort zone. It was the only time that we had the control. He was chasing something unknown. He was breaking the predator's rules in that, and despite trusting me he had potentially everything to worry about.

I only had to concern myself with him and staying within the law.

And of course, there was no girl. To remain consistent in my depiction of this non-existent individual, I tried to visualise what I knew he liked, and repeat it over and over again. I could not go wrong if I ticked all his boxes.

Always mindful of the limits, and that I might have another Wales on my hands in that my superiors could pull the plug at any point, we decided to make the girl real in an attempt to effect a conclusion to the story.

There was still no name nor image but I told him there was a fee of £200 to see her. I was putting obstacles in place in case he really wanted to pursue. I knew he couldn't get the money quickly and I had to see how badly he wanted it.

'Yep, no problem,' was the predictable answer.

He fell short of saying 'I want the girl,' but he said the money was not an issue, which maintained his bravado and would give him a chance to backtrack later if he needed to. But for now, *I* was testing him like I had been probed in the flat job and when my picture was taken in Wales. It was a little marker and he did not flinch.

And still he didn't ask for an image. I find this quite extraordinary and it was the one line here I really did not want to contemplate crossing. It posed all sorts of ethical and moral problems producing a picture of someone who was real but of course, not in the context of what we were doing. Then, what if the photo fell into the wrong hands...it was a minefield, only avoided because he never asked.

We were heading to a conclusion I knew we couldn't reach. The last time I saw him was at his parents. I went through the usual pleasantries, staying and chatting a little while but all the time, knowing that I would walk out of here and my colleagues would be walking in. I could feel no allegiance towards them in that they were silently complicit, knowing exactly who their son was and turning that difficult blind eye.

We had experienced some parents who had turfed their own in but for others it was a difficult call and as soon as I made my excuses and left, knowing that I would never see any of them again and would return to Cleveland Police or onto the next job, our officers swooped and charged him with the little that they could – inciting someone to supply an Under 21 for sexual intercourse. The operational team were also looking at public nuisance offences, because of his method of grooming single parent families.

We knew he was a danger but had very little legal support to put him away. The biggest argument against him was not for a crime that he had committed since his release but for breach of his parole terms and that could get him sent straight back to prison.

I knew we had done a good job. This was different to Wales because I had cast-iron proof that we had saved the futures of many potential victims.

When I reviewed the evidence, I learned that there had never been more people warned on the back of an investigation as with him. He never let on when women whom he had fallen in love with overnight just fell silent.

I suspect becoming accustomed to rejection or disappearing acts just went with the territory and he moved onto the next conquest but the fact that dozens of women were in his life then untraceable is down to the mission. Every time, our support team would offer disclosures to the women who he had been targeting. I was proud that this had been one big swoop without actually the graphic drama and detail of the flat job.

Yet, at the same time two points are important. I do not believe that he did offend in the time that I was his 'friend'. He spent it almost exclusively with me in his free hours so in that respect, I had neutered him, despite his predatory behaviour on his phone during hours in which he could not be out on the streets. He ran out of time. So, I am entirely confident that we prevented by swallowing up his time and by contacting all those targets he pursued – an access that we would not have got if we had just watched him.

On the downside, I also thought it was ridiculous. We had put a lot of time and effort into this job and were still about twelve months away from the legislation changing and here we had an obvious case of somebody who needed to face the consequence of his actions yet if we had laboured the investigation even the slightest bit more than we had then we would have been criticised and that may have been the last straw for the unit.

Indeed, at court, his defence team made claims that my actions were unlawful. They were all over my conduct. I had been here before. It was a classic rear-guard action to pursue the process by which the evidence had been obtained rather than to address the offences. If you could pull the methodology apart then you might never get to the real story. It was a sideshow.

It remains quite hard to explain in the context of the law then and with policing methods in an era before the Internet explosion but there was simply no other way but to put an undercover guy in there. Then, unlike now, we were not in a position to see *all* the messages he was sending in real time. The disclosures we had made to parents were damning enough and if the truth be told, we had actually done him a favour by shepherding so intensely that we had prevented him from offending as he sought to do – the penalties for which would have been much greater, of course.

There was a lot to learn from this operation. Two distinctive methods went straight into the training manual: firstly, this was the first live example for us of targeting the parents of children who themselves become victims of a different kind. He had been grooming me too. Secondly, the mobile phone top-up vouchers that Malcolm would send the parents – not because he loved them as he claimed but of course, to maintain the connection. The use of practical, non-romantic gifts 'because it was the least I can do' were very much his stock and trade.

From a personal point of view, this was obviously less harrowing that the flat job. That particular denouement had spiralled very quickly from what had essentially been the same techniques as here with admittedly very different characters. The key difference was that I had penetrated a loner over a period of eight months to the point that I had become his best friend and we had nipped this in the bud way before the point of offence.

It was difficult to measure one success. Save one child? Well, on this occasion I know the figure to be dozens even if I did not physically set eyes on them.

Malcolm was sentenced to four years. In a way, the defence had won. He was, in essence, returned to prison for breach of his release terms so had to complete the full term that he had originally been handed. It was not my job to be disappointed at the sentence. A different era would produce different results but it was still very worrying that we were *still* not there.

Finally, we did not have much longer to wait much longer.

28

It was time to see Tom, the psychologist. He had been pivotal in my ability to sieve the emotions and fatigue associated with slipping between identities and leaving work at the front door and managing family life right behind it.

Tom was retiring.

This was a blow. I was never the kind of person who was needy enough to be dependant. I could just about deal with what I had seen, knowingly avoided, or all but participated in at the flat, but his skill was not so much in my offloading the enormous stress and drain it placed on me more so the ability to remain a husband and a father.

Talking about it definitely made me more comfortable with the work. It justified everything for me when for regular periods the job was accompanied with suspicion. The longer I was away, the more I was actually immersed in a role or research. That meant, the harder it was for others to accept me on my return.

I did suffer flashbacks for some years after the flat job. These would not be regular but in some way, it was like a victim of abuse on a much smaller scale because I was reliving the experiences too. It did begin to calm down in time. I was one of a very tiny few who saw the predators of this crime in their true light – at first hand, as it was happening.

The only other forum where this work had a place was in the lecture theatre and many potential recruits found it traumatic, often saying their professional self-restraint would be broken. Infiltration was one thing; living the whole process was different. The stress begins from the moment you say yes.

On my return to Cleveland it seemed surreal to be Detective Sergeant.

I could, of course, do the job but had spent so long away and with such unique experiences that in the field was clearly where I belonged but I had to wait for the next job for which would not be too long coming. In the interim, it was back to my Force selecting, interviewing, training and then out in the field managing running operations and supervising all ranks. Nothing had changed at the station in my absence!

Finally, though and significantly, the new Sexual Offences Act was passed in parliament, consigning years of archaic legislation to the history books – and rightly so. It was rare as an officer for you to seek changes in the law. Years later, some cases that you might have worked on would effect ground-breaking policy but I knew from the off that we were up against it and whilst I had no influence, clearly those people who had the foresight to instigate our unit together with various care authorities and organisations across the country who sensed they had missed opportunities, were working towards this for a very long time.

Remember, the previous parameters stretched little beyond acts of vagrancy and indecency in a public place. This time the wording was much more explicit and specific, redefining rape, sex tourism, and significantly changing the definition of 'child' to under 18.

Child prostitution, consent, causing a child to watch a sexual act, pimping for financial gain, plus sex tourism and sex trafficking were on the statute book. Buggery with men and gay sex in a public toilet were new; voyeurism appeared for the first time with specific regard to public changing areas.

Furthermore, people in positions of trust were now on the radar and that also extended to care workers. There was provision for people with a mental disorder too. Notably, too you could see the influence of Megan's Law with offenders having to report to a particular police station for the first time and a general desire to manage Roy Whiting characters living in the community.

And of course, for the first time, online was massive with areas like grooming being redefined whereas previously it had been a vague loophole. Grooming was now an offence even if there was no contact.

Possessing and distributing indecent images was now a crime with additional concern for sexting and the knowledge that such conversations could spread around a school or a community in no time at all with the rise of the mobile phone. By November 2003, we finally had the beginning of a framework that at least brought us to a contemporary position. And this was the year before the big game-changer in social media. Facebook arrived the following year.

How had we suddenly landed here? As the work that I had been involved in for a decade showed the painstaking graft up to now it did not happen overnight and one big sting in America was the catalyst.

In 1999, the ground-breaking *Operation Avalanche* had begun in the USA. That in turn led to *Snowball* in Canada, *Pecunia* in Germany, *Amethyst* in Ireland and *Genesis* in Switzerland. For the first time, there was almost a co-operative attitude even though everyone followed the States. America's *Avalanche* became Britain's Operation *Ore*. To re-cap:

At home, over 7000 suspects were identified, more than 4000 homes were searched leading to at least 3700 arrests, 1840 being charged and 1450 convictions. On top of that nearly 500 were cautioned and 140 children were removed from dangerous situations. In total over 390,000 individuals in over 60 countries were found to have accessed material.

Crucially too, it threw to the wild a huge cross-section of individuals which defied previous stereotypes from military to the church to pop music to academics and civil servants – and worryingly some members of the police. This is the most significant step in the changing of the legislation. When the operation began, officers were largely working to The Protection of Children Act of 1978 which dealt heavily on possession of images. By its conclusion and subsequent court cases that challenged aspects of *Ore*, the Sexual Offences Act of 2003 was the new yardstick.

With hindsight, this legislation that we so craved was the beginning of the end for the unit. Four people alone could not hold this to account, and very soon the laws would have to evolve further because it was very clear that online was now king, not just in this field but in all aspects of life.

If 2003 is the dividing line, it drums home just how up to their necks in it the Midlands ring were – way ahead of the game but also representative of how many more? You could not infiltrate the same group twice. There was no doubt that they could be masters of the new medium and commit even further atrocities. By the time Facebook began to revolutionise all our lives, it was clear that this was where the resource would go. Much of the mentality I had taught in training would remain in officers' armoury but there was a heightening danger that the technology would position me as old school.

The new playground of the paedophile was not the swings and roundabout at the local park or the retail park at an out-of-town shopping mall but hiding in broad daylight with every opportunity to conceal a genuine identity in favour of forging a new one complete with backstories that could be ripped up and re-started time and time again online and for our *guys* that meant no waiting people out over months on end, no bumping into people on buses and feigning conversation, no intelligence that such and such was a mobile phone geek and you could play on that or that so and so like canal boats and you could build a bond like that. Crucially too, the stress of recall and the live moment of face-to-face interaction knowing that a curve ball could come at any time would soon be gone. Keyboard warriors were on the rise and that meant from the police's point of view, the data was all logged and every conversation and interaction was there. You didn't need to carry the character around in your head for months on end any more. It was about to become a younger man's game. You simply just logged back in.

Evaluating this in the joy of the long-awaited legislation change of 2003 is hard. The criminals get smarter too, by the way. The passage of time gives me clarity on this point.

The reality is that the Sexual Offences Act of 2003 only came in partially in the November of 2003 with the rest taking effect the following May. So, it was staggered. Our job would have been much easier if we had got here sooner but it was incredible to have been involved in this work too before the net took over.

Moreover, this legislation was a reaction to what had gone before and that meant that much of this was still on-going as we straddled the two eras. Nor could we at Facebook's birth (and other later sites from Twitter to Tinder) have known the explosion and durability of the new playing field.

The Sexual Offences Act 2003 and indeed the Protection Of Children Act of 1978 still play an active role to this day in dealing with the social media and of course the images that are being possessed and distributed.

In turn, budgets and head-counts are not immediately transferred so in the short term, there *was* still work to be done.

That meant I had one last big job to run. The planning was well under way as the new Act was passed. We always had to carry on with our work regardless of the parameters within which we were operating. Months of preparation could not be jettisoned because of it. Very simply, the crimes were the same and still being committed but the task of convicting was now more straightforward.

And that is why I got another call. There was a huge amount of concern about one particular individual.

Barry was being released back into society.

29

He was a loner like Malcolm. He, too, had connections. Convicted for sexual activity with boys under fourteen, he was generally regarded as 'not a nice person'. Extensive monitoring had been under way for some time – not just from the police but all the relevant authorities too. Even his own family expressed their fears. The authorities had to find a new location for him as the damage he had done in his previous community meant he could not go back there. He had also offended elsewhere.

Journalists were on his tail too and that was a massive problem if I was to ingratiate myself with him. I could not risk a snapper thinking they had their man in the street and finding me in the shot too. One picture could ruin the op and my future credibility. We were a lot further down the line than when I had the same fear with Mr Thailand in Wales. We had come a long way. Anxiety levels were therefore different but equally, raised from the start. That is all I knew. Except one thing. His identity was protected. His name was not Barry.

The request came into my superiors and one force in particular had called to say that they wanted to get a general picture of the situation. Their hunger was to gain evidence and learn. There would be others to follow. Finally, consecutive work when there was so much to be done. And Barry was first on the list.

He was a massive risk. Even his family believed so and they did not even know he had been released. At conviction in the North West of England, he had shown no remorse nor engaged in any treatment whilst inside.

A secret memo had emerged from multi-agency partnerships warning that 'this man will re-offend' and was likely to be involved in several networks in the U.K. I couldn't know if he was acquainted with some of the people I had already been involved with. In total, he had numerous convictions, eight landing him in jail and in 1990s, he received fifteen years for raping three boys under fourteen over a sustained period. He served two-thirds of his sentence.

As the new legislation arrived, it still protected those convicted *before* 1993 meaning that he was exempt from parole or supervision despite the judge who convicted him urging the same new rules to apply to those who had been prosecuted before the cut-off date.

So, he was not on the Sexual Offenders' Register. To our discomfort, it was not just the Sexual Offenders Act that was being updated for the first time since 1956! The modern era meant other areas too had to change and with Barry, the Data Protection Act meant that no image could be released of him, meaning that until he fell onto the radar of a police force, no member of the public could look out for him because they didn't know what he looked like so he could have turned up in Devon or Birmingham and nobody would have the correct intelligence to tail him. His picture could only be released if he were suspected of a new crime or was a fugitive from it. His convictions dated back to the 1970s and he still did not believe he had done anything wrong.

I was therefore in the North of England and now looking at ways to get myself along Barry, who was someone who would always take advantage of free meals and drinks. This only underlines how crucial the research is when you're up against these individuals and so we identified premises who gave the homeless regular food, drinks, healthcare and clothing. Naturally those working in these volatile places deserve a lot of praise for a thankless task for something that would be rewarding but came with risk. Such premises are full of vulnerable people, who can be manipulated by these dominant characters.

Like any centre, it left me walking a moral line. If you are wanting to use the facility as I now did in the role, I needed to show and explain why but I was not going to take up a place that was rightly required by someone who had far greater needs than myself. It was time to get into character again to engineer a meet.

So, I entered and spoke to one of the managers and explained that I had recently moved into the area and that my flat had no electricity…could I use any washing facilities for my clothes and myself? It would probably be only for a few days if that was possible. That was my in.

They agreed so I would use the washing, have some tea and toast for no more than an hour or so every other day. You have to have your wits about you, so not attracting any attention to other guests using the facilities was vital. A new face brings unwanted interest. The odd nod or 'cheers' for picking up the newspaper would suffice. These people were in their own world and for some it was not a nice place.

The staff were great. I was mindful of using the facilities sparingly but they could not do enough for you. I think some of them thought I was posh because the staff would make a big tea urn. Posh people can end up in these places too! Barry, it transpired, did visit this hostel, but frequented others in the area too. We were certainly in the right territory and he was here for his own practical needs – not to fulfil his predatory ones.

I learned that he was frequenting an annexe at the back of a church. This rang deafening alarm bells but I felt it had huge scope to infiltrate even though I was made aware that the group there was unusual, largely made up of lesbians and homosexuals and plenty of children, regularly meeting for tea and cakes and occasionally getting up to read psalms or inviting children to hold up the paintings and drawings they had been crafting while the adults conversed. It looked like a predator's field of play. As an individual, I may look odd trying to join, but once in, I knew I could easily blend in. Barry stood out more than me – slimy, sly and looking like a weasel.

At the hostel, individuals in their own varying states of decline interacted with each other only minimally. At the church, they assumed I was gay and I began to get quizzed by people I really did not want to be put on the spot by. It was one thing being on top of all the recall you needed to infiltrate, befriend and stay consistent with Barry, but nor could I let my guard down with the rest of the group. I could not allow myself to relax just because I was working hard on the known person.

I had suddenly expanded my circle and made myself vulnerable where not just one individual but a dozen or so might run into me in real life or pull me up on something I had said when I hadn't thought it mattered because it wasn't Barry. And the biggest concern there was the children at the church. You did not expect to have remember everything you had ever said to a child but they had the habit of throwing you right off your game with an innocent question which could expose your whole story. At the flat job, I was quizzed multiple times by different people to test me. In Wales, bar one I mostly saw the group socially when they were all together. Now, I was taking on many unconnected individuals at the same time.

The difference was that I was only targeting Barry and nobody else was under suspicion – nor was I aware that they had anything to conceal meaning that they had no 'role' to play. In Wales and in the flat, everyone was hiding behind a false persona. These people were genuine and had no front to act out. That, too, had its dangers because they could be totally natural and might spot someone else who just seemed shifty – and that could be me.

Barry was soon working one of the boys in the church. His moment of entry was simple. When the children were asked to come forward and show their paintings, he would laud one young lad in particular with praise. This was the beginning of the process.

I was totally out of my comfort zone here. I had to feign both my persona and my religion and stepping into the role meant that I would have to embrace that and from time to time they would invite me up to read a psalm. As part of my recall, I now had to chart my religious opinions too and retain some sort of biblical knowledge more than at any point in my life. I backed myself that if I went with the flow and pretended that everything was positive and mostly agreed upon in the world of God, then I would not be found wanting for a stray opinion.

The church, after all, was meant to be a welcoming organisation. I was well aware that within many organisations, certain people liked to hide. The bigger the conglomerate, the easier it was to merge. Recent disclosures against the Catholic Church back this point up, and just like much of the 1980 s football violence was found to be decent middle-class city workers who went crazy at the weekend, many positions of authority within big groups of society that people historically had never questioned were also housing similar individuals. *Operation Ore* and *Avalanche* underlined this point. Barry's track record indicated that he might unwittingly lead me down this route.

But first, I had to crack him so during one of the many intervals for tea and cake, I sidled over to him and made it known that I was in a flat not too far away, which for the purpose of this job would be my home. Obviously, this was close to where he was living and once again and like many of the others before him, he had no transport so the obvious in was to get to the very simple position of offering him a lift and take it from there.

Soon, I was taking him home regularly, building it up step by step asking if he fancied a coffee in the town centres and again roaming the retail parks and main shopping areas.

'Oh, he's cute,' he would say fearlessly.

There was no cat and mouse this time. He just came out and said it, convinced that my attendance at the annexe confirmed that I was gay, and instead seeing me as some sort of competition against his desires which was a totally different dynamic. I had experienced the cagey over months with Edwin, the full-on bravado with Malcolm, and now we were somewhere in the middle where there was almost a challenge to me to match his instincts word for word.

There was no holding him back. Soon, the church meetings meant both the pursuit of the boy and the ability to play me on the way home. I was now often inside his flat where there were no obvious signs of abuse but within those four walls, he knew he was secure and with me comfortable, upping the ante at every possible moment to the degree that once I was left in his kitchen for half an hour waiting for him as the sun came streaming through the windows making it hard to see but proving a welcome distraction from the stench of the place. All these people seemed to live in squalor.

I could see gifts from the boy, namely some paintings proudly pinned on his notice board. That was his prize and so at any opportunity I could, I made sure to praise the boy's artwork so Barry would see he had competition. It was quite clear that he wanted the boy to himself. My feigned interest made him guarded and protective.

As I squinted, he emerged into the living room to ask my opinion. I had waited thirty minutes only to see a man emerge in his swimming trunks – two sizes too small, something which he knew. He had bought them for a boy, or to enhance his manhood.

I don't think I had seen him happier.

'Take a picture of me,' he beamed. 'I want to send it to my friend.'

There always had to be a photo. That Sexual Offences Act was so critical. People think of abuse per se and the wicked acts that it involved but it was abundantly clear from Mr Thailand, through the flat job to Malcolm chatting on his phone to now that the currency with which these individuals did and would always trade was an image. My very first sessions in that sterilised training in London – it was all about the image. Once people started talking about pictures, you knew you were in and the journey began.

You literally unlocked a new level on two fronts. For your own security, when he starts asking you to take a picture of him your mind goes into overdrive that he is going to want one of you and as you know by now, that is a no-go. Secondly, that picture is not a modern-day selfie. Ten times out of ten it is going somewhere. It is taken for a specific reason to send to a particular individual. He had said as much even though he didn't need to. That, of course, brings others into play and opens up his network. The chain begins and the recipient may choose to keep it for themselves, share it or send similar back and you are off. In my experience, it was rare for image exchange to exist just between two individuals. It normally went further. So, I was in. It was vital to get to that photo stage. You just had to up your own game and be ready for that moment when you shyly refused to have your own photo taken.

Sometimes I saw him at the church and others I didn't. That kept it real. It gave me a chance to blend in with the rest of the group who were good people. It gave authenticity to my visits if I was there when he was not but equally it was disappointing and a waste of time if he didn't turn up. The group, outside of Barry, was not a front for anything more sinister though it remained a grey area in that they were only allowed in the annexe and not the church. There was some suspicion or prejudice towards them. I also kept my distance often declining a drink after meetings but agreeing to go to the seaside with them one day just so I could observe Barry.

Once or twice, I rescued him from his grim abode and invited him to mine.

In the comfort of my flat, he was safe except for one thing. My computer.

The machine was logging everything he did and every site he visited, two of which were prominent in my History and displayed young children not too indecently but sufficiently so. Again, I played dumb and with my 'limited' knowledge of computers, let him be the expert. He knew these sites well and where they took him. These were not something he had stumbled across. He too appeared to know his stuff online which was quite revealing given that he spent much of the IT generation inside and he was ageing fast. He knew his way around well. The more he browsed, the more I slowly unlocked him. One to one with images on the computer – that clever, manipulative and secretive front gradually came down.

He told me he had a connection. I was aware of that. They were all linked but then had their own little branches that never knew each other. He was looking to go to the West Country.

'Sounds good,' I replied knowing the area well.

'To a nudist beach,' he added and promptly invited me.

It was perfect for him. Hiding in plain sight again and blending in where nudity was the only option and there was no spotlight on him.

I agreed, of course though I was far from sure that it was the right thing to do. He just saw the meal ticket. I would be the one to drive him there. Experience taught me to say yes now and extract at a later date and I had no concern because it was unlikely his restrictions would give him that window of opportunity unless he was prepared to break them and it had also been intimated to me that Operations were going to wind us up soon.

The thought of myself on a nudist beach was not something I was going to promote. My body was not a temple.

I had spent five months in the company of Barry praising children's art whilst reading psalms and walking half of the British coastline when the inevitable came and the team sat round a table and asked me if they thought Barry was going to offend. To which, I said yes and when asked when, I could only offer 'I don't know'. It was a predictable conversation but we had at least protected the young painter lad who, without our presence, would probably be another victim of Barry's. The expectation had been to gather the evidence in a very short space of time but I knew you could not rush things and we were in transition with the new legislation.

We needed care, though. Save one child. I couldn't let Barry play out for our greater knowledge as per the brief and therefore sacrificing the boy with the pictures in the process, and when, on one of the 20 or so occasions I must have gone to Barry's flat and saw that he had taken almost all of the lad's paintings and kept them there, whilst talking openly to me about him but in a very possessive way, I knew enough was enough.

'He did this picture for me,' he boasted. 'He put my name on it.'

The truth is the boy was drawing for himself and Barry all but stalked him as people mingled around the food area. The child knew no better in his own etiquette or his awareness of anything more sinister in adults but to agree to do so and indeed probably had been brought up to be respectful to his elders.

It was obvious he was lining him up. It was time to act but we wanted to keep Barry live and had to bank on the fact that if we shut him down here, he would re-appear and that my friendship with him would outlive that moment and indeed, I might be the only place for him to turn.

When the disclosure came through discreetly to the parents of the child and word spread quietly amongst the group, I still had to see it through professionally and continued to turn up for a brief period, knowing that he was banned but playing dumb and when I asked of his whereabouts I was simply told that they had found out he was a bit dodgy and would not be coming back.

Of course, I continued to see him briefly and asked him about it to see if his frustration exhibited a reaction where he might let something else out but he just dismissed it. I knew his cold and cunning personality well and that he was angry because he had lost access to the children and that meant he had to start again. He simply told me that he didn't go there anymore.

That meant his world was back to zero. I was left, and he valued me for companionship and the transport and the belief that we were the same ilk. And soon I was gone but we continued to monitor him as I managed my exit from the relationship.

It left me no choice but to miss the trip to the West Country. I simply told him that I had an opportunity that I needed to pursue and I might not be around for a bit. With his, his free transport was gone. He was isolated. Again, I kept the door open, still seeing him on a monthly basis for a short while to keep up appearances but the work was now handed over to surveillance who continued without the interaction. We couldn't know his exact movements and cunning in the same detail but largely working alone, there was a chance he could slip up.

I could have stayed another six months with him and who knows where we would conclude. I also left it knowing that I might drop back into him in the future not just to keep up appearances. 'Likely to re-offend' said the file. He, more than any of the others, stood out as the one I could meet again. The challenge of that dynamic – re-joining a story you had abandoned and all the recall it involved was daunting. All the fears from his release seemed to be justified.

Having spent several months in his company, you build a picture of your subject and he was sly and cunning with eyes that were cold and armed with an uncomfortable laugh full of false emotion. I *can* understand him having no remorse for his crimes. That was who he was. Without doubt, the concern was justified. He would not be too far away from striking again. You had to make hard choices and walking away was one of them. But I knew we had saved one child.

I parked him in a compartment in my mind, knowing that I was wanted straight on to the next group.

It was time for a beer.

30

First was a Private School teacher. Once again, hiding in the system and in a major position of trust. I knew he had already left one such position under a cloud but that it had been hushed up. Schools were very worried about their reputations back then especially as it had been fee-paying.

One boy had made a disclosure against him for indecent assault. The days of Robin teaching were now a distant memory and something he would always hang onto. As standard, I had limited avenues on when and how our paths would cross but it was clear that he spent huge amounts of time at the library.

These are not the best of places for me to infiltrate with eyes on you and obvious noise restrictions.

Intelligence told me that he was a massive real ale fan – this was his area of expertise which was self-taught and that I would play on this time so I stood there near this particular section of books holding a few on the subject looking slightly confused, waiting for him to see a fellow beer lover. It was as easy as that.

I knew he would be there. He was a creature of habit.

The initial advice in training to hone in on their niche area of expertise proved correct every single time. It had to be an ego thing. I knew it was in the mind. Their entire lives were secrets. Their sexual pursuits were unlawful and could not be pursued in open sight. That crushed them and the language of the media and police forces belittled how the public saw them. To be recognised as all-knowing in whatever their field was gave them that big boost which was not therefore available to them elsewhere.

Robin assumed that I *was* an expert on beer when he came over, but I knew as a technique that would not give him the chance to shine so once again I adopted my 'asking for a friend' stance.

'I am having a bit of a do,' I lied. 'And I am looking at real ale pub crawls.'

This was right up his street, pointing out that there was one just around the corner and generally telling me stuff that I already knew. He offered straight away to give me a tour of some of the finest pubs and festivals.

There was a lot of scope for real ale in the North of England. We already had Robin on video filming young boys at tourist locations around the area. It no longer looked out of place for a middle-aged man waving his video camera all around. We are also not to far away from the social media frenzy of the mobile phone replacing the video camera. Consider the eras. A few years only separate what looked odd and what now nobody looked at oddly.

And I was soon – naturally – in a pub with him too and I learned fast that his passion for real ale did obviously extend to drinking it – lots of it. The more he consumed, the less switched on he was and with that his guard came down.

Like many scenarios in this work – every development brought success and risk. Just like I needed Barry to take that photo, it posed threat. Robin spoke freely when he was drinking but of course, he would be indiscreet to other people too. I had to go through the motions but not down a barrel.

I did not see him as any threat, but I knew he was a loose cannon. I could play him all day long but I couldn't know when his tongue would wag and if he would mis-represent me to a third party whom I hadn't yet met but might need to.

We were soon travelling up and down the coast, hanging out at retail parks and amusement arcades and his innuendo and casual mouth just ran away with itself.

'Ooh look at those boys,' he would wail. 'I do love legs. What a lovely sight.'

His drinking also exposed his frustrations. He wasn't happy with his lot. Unlike the original group in Wales who always maintained they did nothing wrong and loved children, Robin felt very hard done by, bemoaning openly to me that he was constantly getting stopped by the police.

This was hardly surprising. He was now on their radar and he did himself no favours, usually dressing very provocatively in outrageous clothing. He complained too that we were now all in the EU and that in some parts of the Union you could have sex with children. Early on, he was one to watch, foolish with his indiscretion and peddling that ridiculous argument.

He knew a lot of people though, and that suggested two things to me. Firstly, that some would have protected him – there remained this cloud publicly as to why he left the Private School job, but I knew. Secondly, some would have had this shared interest. There was now a real possibility that his own casting net was huge.

Robin led me to Mark, a second individual in education, working in the university sector but also widely travelled through Europe where he had been teaching, notably Prague and Romania which, like Amsterdam and now Bucharest, had been looming large on our radar. From this, I am given an introduction to a quiet reserved priest who also had links to that part of the world. His visits there were not of a religious nature.

These connections and their patterns of behaviour were well-established and up to now nobody had been tracking them. It would take years to bring them all in. It was only the benefit of hindsight that could justify how important those two trips to Amsterdam had been. Now, Eastern Europe was becoming the new hunting ground and we needed that knowledge too.

And from Mark came Tim, a well-respected influential figure in administration within Local Authority who played everything diplomatically but had been hiding behind his position for years and we knew was going home to watch a lot of videos. This was one net that was cast far and wide.

He was a keen photographer, but this was his front, enabling him to use his position of trust to fulfil his love of boys' bodies. Whereas Robin always went out in his eccentric clothing, Tim couldn't stop building his collections of lads. I did not want to forge relationships and meet all of these people. I had to keep focus.

You could only run so many multiple identities. So, I concentrated on the vulnerable, but the network never stopped expanding.

'You must meet my friend. He is very loyal like us,' Robin said repeatedly.

And I would be on the phone to a 'friend' in the Home Counties, and then I spoke to an associate in Merseyside. I even met a freelance journalist who had been a casual acquaintance of this network.

This was extraordinary because of the innate fear in my subjects of the media. Police and journalists – they hated and feared their infiltration. Now one was meeting the other. The difference was that he was one of them, and for the purposes of the operation so was I. We were on common footing.

'I have heard so much about you,' I flattered to make him feel important. I wanted to appear credible within his network.

I warned the journalist about the dangers of Robin. He was guarded in his language.

The journalist and myself went on separate paths, but within the world of the child sex offender he was held in very high regard within his circles and considered himself to be a leader and fighting the cause for the beliefs of the paedophile. He had done time, written books and actively promoted the subject. Robin was the key in all the dynamics.

My sightseeing tours – as with Edwin prior to the flat – never ended. It was simply a perfect way to grind stuff out of people naturally. We would regularly go up towards the Scottish Borders and walk for hours around coastal routes, National Parks and museums chatting and stopping for a beer. The sea air cleared his head and that part of the world in its isolation leant itself to that freedom of expression – plus he was in his element with the ale.

From time to time he resorted to type. Generally, he was the most forthcoming and open of all the subjects I worked but sometimes that paranoia and suspicion would kick back in, his memory eroded by the drink.

'How did we meet again?' and his guard would go up once more only for me to remind him of why we were here and that we had first bumped into each other in the library.

While others were still checking me out months down the line when they asked this question, for Robin it was a mixture of both that and the fact that he had genuinely forgotten.

And then he would be fine for a few weeks before self-doubting once more but in between inviting me back to his flat where his guard would completely lapse again, revealing pictures all over his walls made into collages of his previous conquests. In all walks of crime, it was pretty standard that offenders like 'trophies'.

This was his back catalogue and he had a story for each of the boys from a nearby beach to an episode on a canal boat. I knew I had total trust if they were on display to me. How few people outside of the ring could have visited him at home over the years? Almost none, I am sure. His own lack of self-awareness was his downfall.

One police raid and he was finished…no need to look for disks in the fireplace. It reeked of loneliness and emptiness – and unlike the confidence of many of my previous encounters, a struggle to come to terms with who he was. Maybe he was different in that he knew what he was doing was wrong, whilst almost all of the others protested their innocence.

The flat did not stop at images on the wall. He – and I later learned, the others too – had collections of their favourite actors on old VHS video tapes, focussing particularly on compilations of bodies parts and one very prominent scene with the actress Jenny Agutter swimming naked, and a young boy from a tribe. They liked to hang onto these child actors with footage of when they were young. In adulthood they saw different people.

I had to call it in. These were retrospective 'memories' but for the victims on his walls, the past would still be taunting them in their present. He would stare at them fondly. They doubtless were never freed from the pain. It would crush them further in their recovery if they knew that whilst they would not ever meet this man again, he still saw them every day.

We had no choice but to run an enquiry on him and while that was under way I set about cutting him dry from the group, leaving him isolated which would hurt a man whose company had always been milked in his position of authority.

His paranoia and self-pity was only just beginning. The disclosure that followed meant that he got moved in the library and was not allowed near the Children's Section and effectively barred from services within the region.

'They think I am up to no good,' he confessed where others in his position more self-aware than he would have said nothing. 'Obviously, I am not.'

'Obviously you are,' I told him.

In the original trip to Wales, I had experienced being played myself when I went to ask the male in the forces advice only to be blanked as he pretended he had never met before even though he knew I was coming. Now, I set about causing divisions myself suggesting to Mark again that he was our weak link and a security risk with the drink his downfall and he might therefore be our undoing and would he be discreet about this. I was dipping my tow in the water with him trying now to gain his full trust. If I had showed him that level of responsibility and security, then he surely would adopt it too and see me as very credible part of this group.

'I don't like him coming down here too often,' I told him. 'He's a bit full-on and indiscreet. He brings a lot of attention to himself.'

I knew it was important for my own story that I flagged up these concerns. The rest would have no issues about my credibility if I was suggesting that he could get us caught. Through this Mark and I bonded.

In reality, Mark was the most concerning. He typified more than anyone an example of a paedophile who walked fearlessly right up to the line and was so obvious that he did so without suspicion.

He took me to a university campus to see his work. The next bit remains mind-boggling. He was doing a thesis on paedophilia.

It had been a running joke over the years for anyone caught looking at stuff on the Internet that 'they were only doing research'. Except now it was true. Mark was.

I couldn't fathom how difficult it had been for his academic work to get a green light. You could make a very strong case – as much as with our small unit – that it was important work. But it clearly attracted a certain mind – those who investigated it (and few were up to it) and those who were using it as a front. Remember, everybody in this game had to have a front, which you break down before really getting to the heart of their crimes but his was almost unquestionable for being so out in the open.

Somebody higher up had clearly said that it sounded like an erstwhile area to study. Had there been any checks on this kind of work internally at the university? Was it simply a case of suggesting a field and getting a yes or no? Did not the individual have to be thoroughly checked out before the work begun? Apparently not – not then, and probably not now.

I admit. It was brilliant. But wrong.

I knew he was very well connected. It was possible that whilst his name was on the thesis, he may not have been operating alone. It was not the kind of work you could just pull up on a university library computer with hundreds of staff and students around. That, of course, gave him license to operate at home – where most students did their work. University had told him he could look at anything. In turn, that gave him carte blanche to do what he wanted within the framework of a notional dissertation. But it did not mean he was above the law, however naively he played the card. He dropped an almighty clanger with me believing himself to be safe when he told me he suggested that he fancied a boy in his local area.

Some of these creatures cannot resist letting you in once you have passed the credibility test. Look at Malcolm before. One car journey and you got his life story. You hard to work so hard to build that trust but many wanted you to pass it too because then they could share and exhibit that expert gene again. He needed me to be impressed with his cover story. They all needed that little ego boost.

In fact, Mark was so craving company and approval that he told me that his mother whom he lived was going away for the weekend.

'Would you like to come and stay?' he asked.

This was unprecedented.

Of course, I expressed an interest without committing definitely. It was too good an opportunity but I needed to run it by the team and it brought new security risks on a par with the flat job. The only difference was that this time I knew where we were going. I was well aware of the energy reserves I would need to stay in character without a break. Sleep and washing would present challenges. It was a massive risk to the person I was portraying myself as. But it was a new line to cross. Work said yes. I was going to spend the weekend with a paedophile.

31

He began to tell me about Prague and the Eastern bloc Countries.

'You should go,' he urged. 'It's a fantastic place.'

I had no doubt that it was but I knew what he meant by this. The intel told us that he committed abroad but there was nothing on him at home. That Amsterdam trip justified itself once again. So many of these people had done their seedy work abroad. That idea that you could get away with it whilst dabbling in a foreign country was a constant theme – and remember that all the authorities were just catching up, not just Britain. Even though he had lived there, many knew that they could slip in and out for a fortnight and continue almost unmonitored. It was a different matter at home, satisfying your predatory needs around the routine of your day to day life where you created behavioural patterns.

He was an encyclopaedia on the place. He knew too much and that told a story in itself, namely that he had options there. In other words, he had been heavily into the scene.

He listed the railway station as a good place to start. The boys hanging out around it were notorious. A sex shop stood above the concourse and nobody batted an eye. Millions of tourists and commuters must have passed through every week oblivious to what was going on but once you knew, it would become a regular haunt. So much hustle and bustle surround these European destinations from tourists stopping with guide books for photos to Peruvian bands playing at the station. Trains come and go and the people pass through regularly for just a few moments every day. It was as good a place as any to mingle in the melee without arousing suspicion.

But then there was the darker side. He told me to find a very specific place in the old part of Prague.

'You go down into a basement, past these wrought iron gates and press the buzzer. Then once you are in, you find yourself in a square bar with cameras everywhere. Just nearby is a video viewing area and another basement with just a few lights on with a massive beer keg in the centre. There are handcuffs either side of the barrel. Men go there to get tied up.'

He held no punches.

I knew to enhance my credibility further that if we were staying the course on this job, I had to get back out there – abroad. It fact, it was clear that really I should have already gone. We were well aware that he had been teaching English as a foreign language in Romania – a clear in to a youthful aspirational population – and I could have really cemented that bond if I had already made the trip.

'That sounds really good,' I enthused.

But what I meant was thank you very much for the tip off. I will go and enhance my knowledge. If you didn't have the stories and experiences he already did, then you had to let him talk and play the expert whilst pretending to hang on his every word... and we discussed everything that weekend – a whole range of topics but like most people, we would always come back to his favourite subjects and Prague was his number one.

Much of this was adult though, so he was portraying himself as more of a kinky homosexual than a paedophile and remained pretty non-committal until he confessed that he finally had a passion for boys between ten and eleven. He hid himself behind alternative only to then reveal the truth. A weekend in just one person's company does this. You move the conversation on. You share, you reveal your hand.

Alone in his parents' house with nobody listening, he had sewed that whiff of innuendo through his thesis and had led me towards disclosure with the detail in Prague but had never actually put the card on the table. Until now – and of course, people *were* listening in and once he started talking about boys, he was free and relaxed.

Not only did I have to stay in character all weekend, mindful of recall and specifically what I had said to whom in the group, I had two major obstacles to overcome. I had to sleep at some point. And I had the gear on me.

That meant multiple changes. It meant concealing the equipment. It presented a real risk at night time to myself and to those monitoring me. For large periods they would hear nothing then any sound would inevitably jump them into action. But we had to record. It would not look correct in the evidence otherwise, should anything materialise, so you are always thinking ahead and further down the line of any court case and even those long periods of inactivity with nothing really on the tape were important to demonstrate that the scenario was natural. I had very little evidence without it. It was going to be a long weekend and from Friday night until Sunday morning, I had to get past the sleep bit twice.

Worse, he gave me a room with no lock on it. I was grateful for small mercies. At least he had only invited me there to share his world if not his bed.

I needed to sort that door out. I could not have him coming in during the night. Any fiddling with that or sneaking in had to give me a few seconds notice. I grabbed a chair and put it under the handle without really thinking through how I would explain it if I needed to. But it served as a first buffer.

We *did* get on comfortably so daytimes meant I could relax into the character but night only meant small amounts of grabbed sleep so I really had to be at the top of my game to not slip up. I was looking at a 48 hour stretch without the slightest rest.

I had to pace myself too. His computer stood near his bedroom. That made sense. You couldn't know if his mother was aware other than the fact that it probably did not look healthy for a man of that age to still be living at home.

I did not want to bombard him. I wanted him as an ally. He was comfortable talking about Prague because it was abroad and it had passed, alluding to some trouble one of his colleagues had encountered but just leaving it out there without really expanding. You had to be good at reading between the lines and he knew exactly where not to cross. You had to realise when to push for more or just back off. You could ask too many questions and he could withdraw or not really reply and he would carry on talking. Only instinct could guide you. But you sensed, he wanted something more.

If Prague dominated his story-telling then it figured that he perceived they were good memories to him and now he was home, he needed to get to a similar level but was being held back by being in the U.K. That sense that he could away with it was gone, yet he sought its seedy pleasures too. That meant he was still cagey about the computer. I had no doubt what was on there given what he was studying. I think he would have turned it on if it had not been full of images but he didn't ever invite me to look. He left that air of mystery that I knew what he was studying and he wanted me to know but he wasn't going to take me any further. All the time I was making small inroads in amongst normal activity. We watched a lot of TV and went out at night right into the country. There were long periods of just being in each other's company, interspersed with a comment here, a look there and an anecdote somewhere else.

I asked him how the group all met, not that we ever did once together. I never got a definitive answer, suitably vague though the answer was obvious. I knew he had high standing amongst them more so than the teacher who with his own help, I had deliberately undermined. Because of his academic level, the rest looked up to him. I was unclear if they knew about his line of research.

Bit by bit, I drew stuff out of him but was mindful to flit around the conversation. An interrogation was the worst thing you could do and I had to remember the stuff he told me that counted *and* the insignificant bits too. The minor stuff could trip you up. It was as intense as the flat job without that fear in the air. I was living with him and could slip up at any point.

You can see why I do not recall sleeping at all. I would try to cat–nap, setting my alarms regularly on silent to check everything was fine. The house creaked too which was an advantage. I would almost get a warning if he moved before he might try the door.

Of course, I could have no communication with home though Julie knew where I was. She was very familiar with my disappearing acts but I would normally find a way to phone home. I couldn't this time. Instead, I had one back up nearby whom from time to time I would make a short call to say I was fine and he knew not to ask any questions just to acknowledge that he had understood.

The reality is that whilst I may have been on my guard all night long, he was flat out for the count so for nine tenths of the night I needn't have worried but those one or two moments when he might wake up – that was all my restlessness was consumed by.

But I survived both nights and one long day, exhausted by the Sunday lunchtime when I made my excuses to head home. It had not been difficult but I had worked hard to make it easy and keep it so without pushing. I would get him next time or the time after. For now, I had the trust and gave him the credibility to continue promoting me within the group and I knew he was feeding back to them from some of the other conversations I was having too.

I needed to have a chat too with my superiors. And they agreed. I had to get out to Prague.

32

I had to allow a natural break before I could head to the Czech Republic. It would be stupid to have just gone on the back of that weekend, and perhaps odd too to have gone without inviting him with me.

Instead, I took somebody with me who was my welfare and had an understanding of the skill and knew how to handle himself.

The club in the basement was exactly how he had described it – borderline terrifying, certainly intimidating and once inside you immediately think about your exit strategy. You can't leave in a hurry or in disgust. Those same wrought-iron gates won't open for you on the way back if you are doing the place a disservice or look like trouble and I certainly stood out there with my pale complexion in what was largely a Russian world or bearing locals with Romany features.

It was clear from the detail he gave me that he had been here not once but often. He knew the drill and the layout perfectly despite its darkness. For the unaccustomed, getting used to both the sights and sounds placed me on high alert. There was almost nothing about it that was acceptable. It was an eyes in the back of your head place against a soundtrack of wall to wall gay pornographic videos. People were only there for one thing and I could not compromise myself by having a drink tampered with nor did I want to under-stay. My 'minder' and I agreed – a 90-minute stay was a natural length of time without participating.

I needed local reconnaissance too. I couldn't go back and fake something that I had read on Google or Wikipedia. So, like Amsterdam some years twice before, I took bar cards and taxi receipts, museum guides and menus from Argentinian steakhouses. I built up my future archive of knowledge.

I explored Prague ruthlessly as it came out to play in the summer.

Much of it was still very firmly placed in a World War II look. Some of it was run down. You could learn about the old part of town online but it was hard to enthuse about if you weren't actually there.

There had also been a massive flood when the river had burst its banks and you could still see the high watermark one morning as we sat for breakfast in the hotel. This kind of dialogue, though dull, established you. The majority of your conversation would be about the finer details of the city and how you found it, the people, the food etc. The dungeons of torture were the 10% that you only got to after all of that.

And when I returned I told Mark I had been and was grateful for his recommendation and that I had indeed found it a fantastic place and let him know that I had been to that club whist remaining non-committal without being evasive as to what we had experienced there. He quizzed me relentlessly on obscure detail like the old clock in the city centre and boat rides on the river. Now, it was me who was giving him the silent understanding and a chance to read between the lines. I hoped it was another rung on the ladder because I was sure that, as the newest to the group, I was also the last to hear about Mark in Prague, something that was underlined by our intelligence that the entire group were linked to something in that country.

He remained a pretty calm character – a stark contrast to our paranoid provocatively-dressed teacher. He seemed self-assured, hiding behind the research project. If he had not run into me, he would have looked untouchable.

That prevailed until one afternoon when we were out in the car.

So many of the psychological scenarios and cat and mouse relationships had mirrored themselves since I had been doing this work. We tried to condition environments in which we worked the suspects to individuals and locations we largely knew but of course the public was an unknown.

'He's going to hit us, he's going to hit us,' he screamed.

Suddenly we were faced with a drunk driver half-asleep at the wheel heading into us.

Mark looked up terrified as the oncoming vehicle scraped the wing mirror of my car and careered towards a hedge.

'Oh my God,' he wailed. 'You have saved my life.'

'How come you are so calm?' he screamed, still in shock.

'It's just the way I drive,' I replied when of course, I had been on many advanced driving courses.

We pulled over to catch our breath.

'Look, I am going to have to report it,' I broke it to him. 'If I don't, we could be in the shit later on. I will just go to the local nick. There is one just around the corner here somewhere.'

This was a big moment for both of us.

I was undercover and he may be under suspicion. I could not blow the job but I had to stay in character and behave as my persona had evolved and would likely act in this situation.

It was an offence not to stop after an accident, however minor. A third party could have reported us or the other driver, sobered up, and could concoct anything in the days ahead.

I don't know what I expected when I entered the station. I could talk myself through it if I needed to but I really just wanted it to play out naturally and hoped for a quality of service that was appropriate – someone covering the desk would probably think the last thing I want is to do a report of an accident, so you just hope things are done as they should be.

Mark was still shaking in a bad way as the cop re-assured us that there was probably only a slim chance of catching the other driver. And as frustrating as that would have sounded to anybody else, we didn't need him arrested and exchanging too many details.

I needed to come up with a ruse to explain what had happened. I had no surveillance behind me.

'I had better phone my insurance company,' I lied to call it in.

And still he shook so I bought him a coffee and loaded it up with half a dozen sugars. I don't know if his reaction was genuine fear of the potential accident or if entering the police station gave him flashbacks to something I was unaware of or filled him with guilt for whatever he was up to but hadn't yet been discovered. Either is possible.

But the incident enhanced my credibility. He told the story several times over to the rest of the network and his contacts, suggesting I would make a good racing driver when the truth was that I was very experienced but also knew that it was a moment not to deviate from the person he had known and if he genuinely felt gratitude from his survival to allow him to milk that as a new level of trust.

He was not alone. I was walking with Robin up in Cumbria in high winds as we approached a massive waterfall. Heading along the narrow path towards it I urged him not to lean over only for him to slip and grab the rail and avoid disaster, curbing his appetite for the young male for a brief respite as he dried off his clothing.

We had enough on them.

My work was done. One by one we began to dismantle the cell. Tim at the local authority received a conviction for indecent images. He had been getting away with it for over 40 years.

I spoke with Mark who told me that he did not know what was happening but would rather not converse. He had locked down his security. I met a couple of the others and when I asked them what had happened knowing full well the answer, they all just looked at each other. Within the group, there had been little collective communication bar one individual talking to another. They didn't tell everybody everything within their circle.

Then the questions began. I was the newest member of the group so they turned to me with their usual standard question when their paranoia made them retrace their steps.

'Where did we meet again? Why did you speak to me?'

My recall was better than theirs and I set them straight:

'You spoke to me. I was minding my own business.'

If I had not met them afterwards, I would have appeared to be the snitch even though I had been flagging up the weak link from a long way out. It was important to tidy up loose ends. We could meet again.

Not before the local authority official received a conviction.

As part of the Police Force desire to really explore this field, we had uncovered a network that we never knew existed beyond our Real Ale friend being known to us – and it was probably safe to conclude that we had only scraped its surface.

The irony was, that despite the fact that we split this cell up and would be hard pushed to stop them re-emerging and that we had managed to forewarn a university, a library, a local council and a church group, it was me who was in fact going to prison.

33

Rarely did these projects overlap. As the decade that followed showed with online taking over, everything would crash into the next thing from now on and the resource would support it. For much of the last few years, I had done a job and waited, then returned to 'normal' police activity and just sat tight for the next one.

There were false alarms like Roy Whiting and there were huge periods of inactivity when running low-level informants seemed like small fry. Adrenaline surges passed. The craving and the professional drive to 'better' the flat job and close down more than a handful of individuals at a time never left you. You knew it was still out there even if you were not assigned.

The moral onus to save one child always remained and whilst you could never keep a tally in your head and the drama of The Midlands or the subtle manipulation of Barry and the lad with the paintings enabled you to see first-hand an individual minor at risk, the unknown number of children, whether as an image on a screen viewed by these individuals or children that they had kept from us, remained a figure that we could only speculate at but we knew was way out of control.

Hence – periods back on my 'real' job, climbing that career path to rungs that I never really took on, were often frustrating. I simply had to wait until I got the call.

As the previous operation was being wound up, I was being alerted to someone in prison who was a risk. This was a massive problem and will probably concern you that an individual serving time could still be a danger. It should come as no surprise.

Early release to a safe house with curfews in place was intended to be reward for good behaviour and a deterrent to those offenders who were given a chance back in the real world but whose re-integration was being managed. Four hours a day or so like Edwin was enough to see if they could merge back into the real world or fall foul of the slightest distraction reeling them back into their bad habits.

The only downside of this staggered rehabilitation was that it probably followed a period of long contemplation in prison where urges and desires were reaching boiling point. That meant that those who constantly re-offended began that process of plotting from the inside and in Edwin and Barry's case, that readiness to re-join a previous network once the coast was clear was prominent.

The individual that drew me to prison was near to the end of his sentence for convictions on boys. He had placed an advert in a gay magazine. Obviously, post, phone calls and online are monitored from inside and everybody knew that. There was the whiff of police corruption and indeed prison corruption. The system was not always transparent and honest and you knew from history that some stuff got through. A criminal would not stop trying but unless severely deluded was he genuinely expecting a reply?

He got one of course. I wrote it.

Then he wrote back to me. Pages and pages. Unstoppable rubbish. Getting carried away in his mind, mentally checking out of that cell and walking back on to the streets for further re-offending. It was an odd process. Knowing the risks of that letter being intercepted, he still did it.

Then when I began to correspond with him, his own security went out the window at his sheer delight that somebody had answered the ad. It was a hopeless intellectual circle from desperation with risk to elation with equal danger.

There was no point to any of it from his point of view unless his mind was so messed that he saw no harm in it. So close to being released, he was foolish enough or out of control to flag himself as further risk and must have assumed that he had got away with it to have received a reply.

The truth is that he did draw attention to himself as a problem by placing the ad. Otherwise I would not be driving to the South Coast of England.

I had written little to him other than 'how's things?' or 'look forward to meeting you' but it was enough for him to over-engage. I could have been anyone, nor again did he require a photo.

Soon enough I was passing coastal attractions that took me back to my childhood. As you saw the signs ahead with the landscape changing from motorways to A roads and a slower pace of life flanked by the countryside, I was all but heading home to meet him.

Never in a million years could I have imagined that my Dad's drive to get me career focussed would end up heading to court a paedophile inside prison. Nor could my Dad have second-guessed that and as I headed towards my latest rendezvous, I realised that I had never really told either of my parents what I *really* did. You always hoped that those closest to you would be proud that you had even saved one child but would probably ask to go easy on the detail. Whereas for me, that detail was everything from the planning, the execution and then the memories that it left. But they never really knew any of this.

I am conscious of my surroundings and some eyes are on me. You expect people to look at you or nod, but conversation is minimal. Waiting outside the prison gates a queue forms, everyone holding their visitors pass. I come as a member of the public. The gate is opened by the guard and I follow the line and look ahead focussed, without eye contact or looking around.

Suddenly now I am in a Portacabin-shaped building with a cloakroom with everything visible to the guards. Everybody is ushered to their seat. No one speaks which leaves an uncomfortable silence. It feels awkward. Then they are ready for us.

I walked into a mixed prison – not just for sex offenders. It was like going into a blind date in a controlled environment. All the sex offenders had their visits at the same time. I was surrounded by them. This was concerning work and caused the planning team countless headaches because there could be *no* planning. I was not known to the prison staff. I was not briefed as to anyone else who might pose a threat in there and the one predictable thing about entering such an environment was that it was unpredictable. It was a huge risk.

Something could give at any point and wardens might turn a blind eye based on something previous that I was not party to. There was little my back up team could do from the outside. It was not as though they could storm the flat, for example. I had to rely on my wits and count on no disasters.

Inside those four walls were enough challenges to keep a force busy for a lifetime. I was focussing on this one individual. It seemed lost on him as we met that the chances of anyone replying to his advert of sane mind were pretty slim.

'You're not what I expected?' he began.

'What did you expect?' I replied.

Answer a question with a question.

He was over-bubbly, predictably frothing. The exchange of letters had driven his nervous state to this culmination. I said little. He had a mental image of who I was in his head. That was often the way before you met somebody but for an offender it was pretty standard to build up a picture in your mind when the physical portrait of that individual mattered less than the control and power you were exerting in tandem with your own predatory needs.

He had just five months to go. I think he felt invincible. That he had done his time and was off the radar. With the new legislation, we were finally in a better position to deal with him. He was preparing for life on the outside. If he had a network, it looked like he was fast-tracking his way towards it.

I had arranged two more visits prior to his release, so the processes were the same and the levels of apprehension remained. These meetings were very edgy as though every encounter bore no relation to the previous but a necessity in order to bond this unlikely friendship. We had to anticipate his next move and keep tabs on him once he was out banking that I would be his first port of call.

On his release, I met him very early on. Every time, it meant a long drive back home from the South Coast with no easy way or direct route. These were long journeys laden with traffic. Julie knew I would be some time. He believed I lived 'not too far away'. This was almost the longest journey you could do in the U.K. beyond Berwick to home in Penzance but these individuals were such a risk and my work was so specialist that there was not the option of finding a local me to take on the job.

So, however many times I had to make the trip, the mantra remained. Save one child. This meant I was regularly strolling around new coastal attractions, retail shopping malls or taking boats out to sea, just like I had walked the coast previously and still going through the motions of breaking this person down mentally by gaining trust.

Crucially too, the last few years had taught me that the first encounter these individuals have when they taste freedom creates an unprecedented opportunity to build that.

Perhaps giddy with their newly found freedom and their guard not quite up yet, people like me are a gift to them. With the shared interest and the transport, I was too good to be true – because I wasn't. To be the first person to be trusted on the outside placed you in pole position.

Penetrating his world a few months down the line would mean evading others whom he had aligned himself before you and that meant the vetting, the scrutiny, the proving yourself all over again. I had gone to visit the guy in prison specifically to avoid this and now I was in. The police work began, in effect, while he was still in custody.

He never made any advances on me. I recognised this trait now. I was meal ticket rather than the main course.

'You're not my type,' I told him early on.

'I know your type,' he replied.

It had in fact been pretty standard that these characters had no design on me but their intentions towards me were simply 'common ground'. I was not the focus of their desires but I was the facilitator potentially. The insinuation that I might be was part of their cat and mouse.

In his eyes I may also be able to provide boys from my 'network' as well as being the confidant and chauffeur.

I turned out to be neither. Within nine to ten weeks, he was back inside, arrested for breach of his release conditions. Indecent images on his phone condemned him.

He must have thought it was all going so well. I didn't go back to visit him but I don't suspect he spent the next few years dwelling on our lack of friendship. His mind had been so easily bought that if anything I suspect he wondered if I had been caught too. I didn't need to see him again to tidy this up.

His case is not so much landmark but as it coincides with my own career, a definite marker in that it falls post Sexual Offences Act of 2003.

The technology and Cybercrime were already racing away leaving clear daylight between that legislation and the criminal reality but it did at least give us the reward that we had been silently aiming towards pre-2003 and were now armed with a whole range of powers that meant there was no chance individuals like this man could offend again.

They were monitored pre-release, intercepted as the moment approached and they very simply handed back in once they were out if they offended or broke parole terms. There were no obstacles any more that a defending barrister could throw at us. We could not be done for enticement or 'entrapment' type slurs.

We did not change any of the methods that we had always used in preserving the evidence in that we were rock solid in showing that the individual was committing the crimes without being seduced. The difference was that we now had a contemporary range of powers. The digital generation no longer had to rely on busting people under an antiquated Vagrancy Act where he may be deemed a public nuisance.

The Protection of Children Act 1978 did and does cover the

possession and distribution of images. To this day it still plays an active role that operational online investigation teams use in dealing with the predator online.

In that respect, this simple but patient and unique operation was hugely significant. It was my first success of the new era and it meant that Law Enforcement Agencies could really begin now monitoring multiple targets with increased powers.

On a personal level, that came at a cost.

34

It's 2004 and I have done my last major job. From time to time there will be calls asking if I can go here, track this person there but suddenly almost overnight, the forces are ready for the legislation even though the nature of its timing means that we are always playing catch up.

The 2003 Sexual Offences Act is the border crossing into the new era. It brings my work up to date but also positions me as out of date. That one to one jockeying for position, of intercepting a character in a 20-minute window in a place I don't know in a bid to befriend them over a very specific detail and then carrying all that mental stress with you for the duration however long that might be…it was over.

Now, people with better tools and a more robust set of powers were about to do – if you like – the same kind of work as I did but in a different playing field, meaning that they didn't need those communication skills on a one to one level but they could sit in front of a computer or laptop with different, and equally as worthy techniques running multiple identities over numerous offenders of a variety of crimes (not just in this work). They did not need to get their hands dirty in the same painstaking way, but their hands were soon muckier than ever as the Internet floodgates opened.

The new Act and increased budgets were welcome and long overdue. Writing this over a decade later, it was essential that this happened – and yes, I was brought up to police in a different era. I am also very proud that the work my colleagues and I did brought us to this conclusion, albeit with other variables too.

Whilst individuals like Roy Whiting made politicians and media certain that the rules had to change and then social media sent them spiralling out of control, I know that our work was pivotal in putting the police's case forward for the change in the law.

The original mantra of save one life remained. We also had to do so one by one. To have rescued just one individual made it worthwhile. For me the figure was at least 50 and who knows the sum total once you cut these people's supply off. The new era would save many over a continued period of time. What was glaringly obvious to people like George and myself were not so much the 'successes' but the incompletes.

If you look at Wales and the whiff of sex tourism, the new Act covered that. If you considered the times we had done so much of the work and were then asked if we would get a result or not, it looked like a failure when in fact the business of policing (such as costings) sometimes got in the way. Add to that, if you consider the narrow escapes and the disclosures that we were able to make after the painting and decorating job then to me it all adds up to one thing.

We did save more than one child. Straight away, that is a happy conclusion. The picture, however, is clear. At some point when Bill Gates, Steve Jobs and Mark Zuckerberg were re-defining the landscape, somebody much higher than my boss whom I have probably never met, must have been making a case saying that we have four or five guys in the field working on this stuff but we have no resource, they can only go so far, and they are trying to nail people under laws that are 150 years old.

Despite the much-needed change, I do not believe anybody – certainly in the police – had any concept of how big the new parameters were or how fast it was spiralling out of control. It was beyond computers. Mobile phones were equally as dangerous.

With the clarity of the years passing, I can see now that what we did not achieve was as significant from the police's point of view in the changing of the legislation as what we did accomplish.

For every flat job, there was a tower block somewhere where the lift did work. Many still had an escape route.

Despite the changing of eras and the investment finally in digital, I knew and my bosses understood too that my best role in the final years of my police career would now be in passing on the knowledge. I had always seen this as a given, having taken my lead from George whose desire too was as much borne out of the unique experiences that he had had as the need to find another him and in the end that proved so difficult that, after me, there were never more than another three in the unit.

Knowledge and experience, even when the parameters move as drastically as they did towards keyboards, could never be substituted. Anecdotes and real-life operations would always remain a narrative of police forces whether you trapped somebody in cyberspace or shot them dead in broad daylight.

And so, my new role began officially or evolved naturally into even more training in charge of the low-level operatives. It is worth remembering that in the early days of the Internet, many offenders were wary of the unknown of how you might get caught online, having heard horror stories from other people in the network, which totally justifies the character I assumed feigning computer ignorance to befriend these predators. Some did stay away.

Furthermore, there still remained those people who were hard to trace, avoiding the radar of the taxman, and running multiple mobiles. The world of contraband and dodgy dealings liked to play in the open as much as cyberspace.

That meant that my experience was still critical. The shift − in the hunt for the sex offenders − was now online but the techniques that took me towards that role still had total relevance in the undercover gangster world from where I had come.

Business was not always online for them.

Arms and drugs were still coming in through the ports; much property and a huge percentage of the car industry was still dodgy. Often, much of this ultimately led to the bigger crime. Everything I had learnt and experienced was now focussed on re-telling my story so the next generation could re-write a new ending. At that meant at home and abroad.

I was invited back to Romania to address the officers there and whilst that was an honour created by the whispers from the flat job, it also stands firm in the memory because of the context it gave. Here was a nation with much street life. In that, I mean prostitution, trafficking and children living rough. Many of these people did not officially exist which made the problem worse. Some infants were being bought and sold. This was, like Amsterdam, Prague and Thailand, a key place to visit but for different reasons.

The other three had been about the knowledge for getting into character. This was about comprehension of their parameters from a police point of view and there was little you could understand. Before me stood officers committed to work akin to what I was doing but with not a hope of carrying it out.

There was a such a blind eye culture and an acceptance of this street life − not dissimilar to the unofficial favelas exposed later by the Brazil World Cup of 2014 − but not quite on a par other than for the realisation that a huge populous were living by their own rules, which were no rules, and often with the state oblivious to or ignoring their official existence.

So, when I cursed the Vagrancy Acts and bemoaned the tortoise-like speed with which the Sexual Offences Act of 2003 came in, I was mindful to remember that in the UK we had been at the top of the game with no resource when here was a force nowhere near it with equally less to operate with. People in the UK were targeting some aspects of Eastern Europe and their own officers were powerless to intervene, so behind was the culture. In short, we were dealing with many people who did not officially exist.

For a moment when you are in the country, you put aside your frustrations back home and realise that it is so much worse in places like Bucharest. Then, of course, you return home and you can only play the hand you are dealt and that meant that in 2003, we got just about up to speed and there was no turning back.

The officers in Romania, some of whom had escaped crime to enforce it, would look with envy at where we were back home and where I had come from would have been considered advanced compared to what they were facing. The contrast was stark: I had been tracking people convicted and about to re-offend; they struggled with no powers to stop what they could plainly see in broad daylight without even having to work for it.

Of course, I sensed that I was coming to the end of my time in the field and that also meant that I was becoming much more objective about the flat job. As the years had gone past, something that was hard to discuss except from de-briefings and with the psychologist became the mainstay of my presentations because it gave me credibility in front of a new, young audience who often had not done their time, so to speak.

Who was this slightly older, matter-of-fact guy speaking to us? He didn't look like one of us. What can he possibly tell us? Is this granddad telling stories from the war again?

But the facts spoke for themselves and on that they were hooked. The story remained the same – never embellished. The ending always shocked people but the real lessons were in the building of the relationship, and the communication skills. The afternoon in the flat would never be anything but horrific and placed a tough moral compass in front of many people coming to my presentations but the key to the police work really was in the detail that got us there.

Indeed, nothing had changed in the history of the police. By nature, endings were often dramatic and regrettable but the detail, patience and ability that took you there were the elements to cling to.

Every time I told the flat job story, I knew that it was my kind of policing. I was a face to face officer. Perhaps, it is generational, but the new online work was not for me. I needed to be in the field or inspire those through teaching who might have that work ahead.

Crucially I was being utilised to role-play to organisations who interviewed child sex offenders on Critical Operations courses, this was an initiative by C.E.O.P. (Child Exploitation and Online Protection) in how to *interview* the kind of individuals I had been befriending for the last decade. Only a select few had this experience and nobody outside the unit had the ability to contrast the offender being interviewed with who they had seemed to be before arrest. I was in that unique position, learning their every cunning cagey mood and techniques from sending mobile phone top up cards to hiding behind the university yet knowing that when under caution they became a totally different person who believed they had done nothing wrong but also had the power of recall too that I had worked so hard on perfecting in managing every step of my relationship with them.

Throughout my whole involvement befriending these predators, I knew that any aspect of our relationship would be questioned in the moment I would least expect it. That meant that all though they were often prone to moments of stupidity, they were also very clever and could play the game as well as me. In the interview scenario, that manifested itself.

I would trot out all the lines, unrecognisable from the clear, calm individual who perhaps the same day had been guiding them step by step through training. It would be two of them against one of me. I would play it deliberately difficult, trying to make them uncomfortable, looking them up and down as Malcolm would have done, mentally undressing his interrogators. The students needed to understand that this end game was the toughest psychological battle of them all. I learnt from those who I had befriended.

In playing that role in training, the only area that did not reflect the experiences that I had was that now there were a much broader set of options in the law to prosecute and therefore question whereas all of those whom I brought in were largely 'protected' by the limitations before the 2003 Act.

For me, nobody specifically said the game was up. Jobs were coming in only irregularly and not on the scale that they were. Nor did anybody say that we had done a good job. It was not that kind of culture. But I knew that Law Enforcement Agencies was going one way and I was heading the other.

It was only really the arrival of that letter in 2006 which Julie opened which gave context and a defining lasting sense of clarity to what had gone on.

35

There were still moments when the phone would ring and they wanted me specifically. In 2010, one such call highlighted a problem of the new era.

We had become aware of an individual specifically looking for a child. He could have found this on the Internet. For many, this was a risk and the irony of any such cases being so public and widely covered by the media meant that it shut down other networks and sent many underground.

This job came and went in a flash. The man concerned was due to call me back. I waited ten minutes and there was nothing. This did not normally happen. Of course, for all the 'successes' one knock-back makes you question your whole demeanour. What had you said on the previous conversation that made him nervous? Had you lost your touch? Or was it something totally obvious and explicable? I had always backed myself but everything was an equation and you never knew what was happening at their end so I never spoke to the guy again. But this was rare. They nearly always called.

The problem was that it showed Police Forces that there was still this underworld. While everyone was concentrating on and policing cybercrime, we still had an element of society where people did not exist.

The lead had come to us from a prostitute.

As hard as it may be for people to understand, often there were respectable relationships between policing and sex workers and even for the prostitutes, there was a line and from time to time their moral code kicked in which meant that blind eyes were turned to paying for intercourse, but when they, in 'intimacy' acquired knowledge that was borderline they tacitly passed it on. This was not the first time.

So, whilst we were grateful for this, it exposed that even though the

Act of 2003 had new provision for sex workers and trafficking, the focus on it in Britain was minimal. Prostitutes still 'roam' the streets to this day and the police stay clear but that industry was not really an online business and those individuals who did not want to do their seedy work on the net were still out there in a world that was largely un-policed.

It was disappointing but the work, outside of the training, was now confined largely to this. And there was a difference. If I wanted to do the work I had always done, I almost had to rely now for tip-offs on people who were undercover themselves such as prostitutes or people who were unknown to us, which suggested despite the fact that you could track anybody anywhere online, those who fell below the radar would remain there unless we had a stroke of luck and there seemed no obvious policing method to counter this.

What happened in Rochdale in 2008 and 2009 where racial tension and sexual exploitation conspired to torture at least 47 girls resulting in convictions in 2012 and subsequent TV dramas exposing a system of failure in the social service meant that there were still ways and means, and elements of society who saw no wrongdoing.

There remained non-Internet sexual offences that required the original type of work and so-called 'minority groups' continued to operate in broad daylight – in this case largely at a taxi firm and takeaway service – as though the Internet had almost removed the spotlight from 'traditional' grooming and exploitation when this was an open secret and one of the biggest cases in sexual exploitation that the UK has ever known. For Rochdale, also see Oxford, Peterborough and Rotherham. The list was endless and that is only amongst those who have come to light.

I could view the non-return of the phone call as a disappointing way to end or a mark of success that our work had ended up here. Either way, it confirmed to me that my future was in training.

By 2010, I registered a business to that effect and began touring the country giving speeches to many sections of society from foster organisations and care agencies. I started working closely with organisations like Barnardo's, the legendary British organisation most prominently associated with orphan children but now also dealing with their own issues of Child Sex Exploitation and their newly formed project SECOS.

I was able to see at first hand the other side of the equation and how the work that we were able to achieve and the huge parts of it we could not, hit home hard because it *was* close to home.

SECOS was an operation unique to Middlesbrough – Sexual

Exploited Children On Streets. The average age in the area of those who were sexually abused for females was between twelve and thirteen. Some were younger. A few had been imprisoned by their perpetrators. Many had ended up on the streets.

The organisation believed that exploitation was becoming more organised and sophisticated with networks of older men grooming *and* trafficking. It felt like a mixture of Wales and the flat job but now the technology that empowered us to work smarter also did the same to them. Through SECOS I was able to explore in more detail the emotional consequences for the victims. Children who had made disclosures and fed that back to the police. I had read many victim statements over the years but it was always in a detached manner.

Now, I could see at first-hand what happened after the police's operation was done. Much of the real work then began repairing the minds of the victims – something I found intensely rewarding partly because you become almost immune to the emotions when you are working this field for years. You wonder from time to time what happened to the boy in the flat but you don't lay awake worrying about it. Removed from your official role, you remember why you did it and have a rare opportunity to see the end project, albeit damaged.

Decent systems were now in place whenever a police sting took place, with social services and councillors involved in the operations. The focus had really moved onto the victims more than the predators to such a degree that there was almost an after-care service with teams going into the communities in the days that followed a sting. Your involvement (beyond giving evidence from behind a screen) had always ended at the arrests. Work with projects like SECOS completed the circle.

It gave me an opportunity to start moving on too. As I promoted the work to younger people coming through and worked with organisations like Barnardo's and Foster care agencies. I also began putting myself out there for me.

I valued hugely the opportunities with Barnardo's as a volunteer, project worker and finally as a trainer, and during this process, I met Wendy, the manager of the SECOS project who for three decades had been promoting the fight against children being sexually exploited. She could see that my experiences were unique and from the other side and the knowledge that I had acquired just reinforced that, not only were children being exploited but also those parents or carers who had vulnerabilities, therefore enabling the sexual predator to groom the adult, so they would be unwittingly used as a barrier and rebutting any concerns from those outside looking in and only seeing good in the predator. Shared knowledge for both of us was invaluable.

This was to be the new me and on 29 April 2011, that day finally came.

By that point, anyone who had been with the police three decades was nailed on to go, though I didn't really want to. Even though I was not blind to the changes constantly evolving round me, there was no sense after the Prague reconnaissance trip that it was the last trip.

Even though resource was all online with most forces now employing at least 500 or so registered specialists and post 2003, it opened up so many more possibilities, I always felt there could be at least one more job. It followed to me that whilst the groundwork of the paedophile could now be hidden exclusively behind a keyboard, offline meetings were still taking place and the logical conclusion of Internet grooming was inevitably a meeting.

Furthermore, policing the Internet for child sex offenders *is* an impossible task. The speed with which sites are created and utilised and can also disappear really mean that the new generation of cops are fighting a losing battle.

In my time we did experience people right across society being sexual predators of children and the ages of the offending were not a stereotype restricted to being over fifty. Some were as young as twenty. And yes, we did have those victims who had been groomed so well that on reaching the age when the predator's interest would wane, would be duped further in bringing other potential victims into the network's lair.

There was also the new territory of children on children. Sexting, and the sharing of images around schools and colleges changed the landscape of the offender with a devastating effect. The mobile phone became the universal facilitator. People from all walks of life were now being caught. The guy at the Local Authority represented many more. The press surge too that began with Sarah Payne right through to Jimmy Savile also played as big a part. The public were engaged. Many who seemed normal on the outside were exposed as being monsters within.

Charities nursed victims and as one spoke out, it gave confidence to others to do the same. Savile was the greatest example of this as victims who had never met found comfort in each other and felt that they finally had a voice, and significantly, at last were believed when previously they had no power.

Global communication amongst forces was still not where they needed to be. The Philippines, Cambodia, Thailand and parts of Africa remained a huge worry. Sex tourism, though covered in the Act, remained difficult to police because of the speed with which people travelled through countries and the lack of permanence 'tourists' would hold in that location.

I am aware of one of my colleagues from the Met regularly travelling across Asia forging relationships with law enforcement and welfare organisations looking at prevention, welfare, and education. It was a slow process but it had at least begun and over some decades we had come a long way from those early chats with George and a unit of just four people.

Meanwhile in the European Union, the age of consent remained lower than in Britain. I still clung to the belief that if the right job came, they would call. But they didn't.

There were repercussions though for all undercover work. In the years that followed the Pitchford Inquiry several covert operatives were exposed as having gone beyond their remit. Some had sexual relationships and children within the political groups that they had infiltrated.

Getting it wrong was a major problem – 26 convictions were quashed and substantial compensation paid out. Notably, the Rawcliffe Power Plant in Nottingham has tarred many covert operations with the same brush.

My methods were never subject to this scrutiny and when I foresaw such retrospective trouble ahead I had withdrawn. Now, I had done so for the last time.

It was over. My career came to an end. To show for it, I held numerous commendations from Chief Constables, Deputy Chief Constables, Assistant Chief Constables, plus letters of appreciation from law enforcements throughout England and Wales ... not to mention more than generous words from officers to whom I had given presentations on the specialist subject of infiltrations of the child sex offender officers working in European Counties.

It had been exciting, even thrilling and I wouldn't change a minute of it.

So, after over 33 years' service, I handed in my warrant card and left the Police for the final time that April day. Without fuss or fanfare, I was done.

'We wish you all the best,' a supervisor said.

And I turned and left.

I was not one for leaving dos and because of my network it would have been impossible to organise. Logistics would make it impossible. I did want to do something so organised a charity golf day with around 110 people joining us, raising £1100 for Breast Cancer. Police and golf seem to come hand in hand and for some it was the only real opportunity to find out a small amount of what I actually been doing all these years. Many never knew or certainly not the extent of it. It was a jaw-dropping final day confession but one that Julie and I saw as important and for a charity we cared a lot about.

The last laugh was hers too as she tracked down one of my senior officers. It was the very same Mark whom I had secretly visited when I received my letter from the Queen. He too had now retired as a Detective Chief Superintendent and kindly rose to say a few words. He knew more than most. But even at the final farewell, he never really expanded on the little that people knew. Right at the end, we stayed in the role.

I was speechless, truly overwhelmed. I could only manage a garbled response. Julie had kept this quiet, but it was great that she had done so.

That hunger for a new challenge was what to do next, too young to stop and do nothing. My father had been wise and correct to suggest that this might be my future. It was now also my past.

To my knowledge the flat job has never been repeated. As the years went by, more and more people got to know about it from presentations I gave and I became more comfortable in time, sharing increasing detail of it to those who heard it third hand from someone else.

My work with foster care agencies and Barnardo's meant that I was promoting more prevention and awareness so I felt I was trying to make a difference in my new world whilst showing discretion with the language and tone that you use, and also learning to be me again beyond this 'other person' which was the front for the work.

Explaining to individuals the danger of public places and the targeting of single Mums was a message that was slowly being heard – a situation not helped by the fact that many organisations working extraordinary hours survive on kindness and limited financial support. Charities find it particularly hard. Good will can run out in the end.

That paranoia over *Panorama* and equivalents could finally subside too now I was out of the role. I began to work briefly with a journalist called Tazeen Ahmad, an experienced freelancer who is passionate about the subject of the child sex offender and appears on Channel 4's *Despatches*. She was very experienced in child sexual exploitation, and reported on a huge investigation in Derbyshire.

I finally went public in a *Sunday Mirror* column which only really scratched the surface, but the substantial donation to the SECOS project was a great motivation for doing so. This was a massive moment for me and something I pondered for a long time fearing a backlash.

There was none. Even though many of these individuals were getting smarter, so were the public. The message was getting through.

23 NOVEMBER 2006

I am bound to say I was just doing my job and at no point in my career was it a motivation to end up here. In fact, I was probably still processing much of what had happened even though I was probably two years past the point at which my skills were regularly being utilised.

I knew very few people who had gone before the Queen. I was clueless as to what to expect and staggered I was here but the train journey from the North East gives you plenty of chances for reflection and clarity. A million opportunities to stare out the window as the countryside moves into suburbia on the approach to the capital and in the reflection back, I saw the Edwins, Malcolms and Barrys of this world, and still my family could not see what I was glancing back over my shoulder… towards.

I couldn't occupy myself with what those characters were doing now – inside prison or out – but I knew that they were the reason I was here. My recall never left me and small details would playback but I think stepping off that train at Kings Cross finally allowed me to draw breath. I would never see these types again and now was protected by the Queen who was about to recognise what this had been really about.

And yes, I was proud but it was a sentiment that was only arriving now. Without exception, at the conclusion of every individual job, my only emotions were 'job done' and now 'let's get home'.

This one day in London gave me finally a chance to gain a broad perspective that even Tom the psychologist couldn't bring. I think it drew a line.

It also completed a circle because when we arrived the previous afternoon, I took the family to The Ritz for tea to see what all the fuss was about. I had been here once before as a young officer with a detective when we were at West End Central. It gave me perspective and helped measure the years in between. Beyond that, nothing had changed. It remained full of Americans and was still expensive!

So the morning came, and I had a brief sense of protocol but these are one off moments in life where you just assume you will say little at and wait to be moved on. For all the tranquillity that I had tried to bring to the role over the years and then transport home so as to not contaminate our life, I felt a little queasy and a tiny bit giddy. The reality is there was no reason to do so. The work was being acknowledged by the highest in the land. The worst was well and truly in the past.

But there is no benchmark for the day and its surreal nature. I am not ever attracted to celebrity and frankly he could have been anyone but as we exited the hotel to take a taxi towards Buckingham Palace, the chef Gary Rhodes was also doing the same. We were obviously both heading to the Palace. Few are dressed that way at that time of day in London. It was comforting to see someone else wearing similar and so that forms a silent bond that whatever you have done in life and whomever your public perception is, it did not matter on days like this. We were a club of two.

We pulled up around 11 am and must have waited for around 90 minutes. Time stood still again of course but at least this time, it was the right reason. All around me, a military operation was under way. Whoever was doing the presentations today was seeing 125 individuals. Outside busloads of Japanese tourists were taking pictures without really knowing why.

We entered through the main gates and then via an inner entrance that nobody sees, turning into a square courtyard. Few have only glimpsed beyond the controlled images on the TV and even I was surprised to see how massive it all was. It is safe to say that I was walking in a trance.

It was time to set foot in the building, greeted by red carpets and a man at the top steps directing those receiving awards to the right and their family to the left. I would not see them for some time as they made for the gallery to look down on the ceremony.

As they offered soft drinks I *did* feel nervous exuding a rare lack of calm. It just takes over you. You speak rubbish for small talk with those in a similar situation and people give you rubbish back because you are nervous. My conversation was limited to inane chatter like 'this is a nice place – look at the paintings' and everywhere you look you see frame after frame. I was not necessarily a connoisseur but every wall was adorned with endless art.

Your eyes follow transfixed, just as your walk had done bringing you here.

Your spell is broken by the calm booming voice of a Lord Lieutenant who has drilled this scenario many times interrupting a silence only previously broken by nervous murmur. He began to call names in tens alphabetically. Now, it became real. Ahead you could see those before you receiving their awards on a TV camera – some familiar faces and many unknown but we all shared that sentiment that doing our work brought us here and that on no given day did any of us really see this as the goal. Some like me will have also been mooted some time ago and believed the moment had passed and then just carried on with their life, never sitting around waiting for a gong. It was the job that defined you, not this day.

The only comparable experience in terms of nerves or expectation as you wait in line can really be waiting for the dentist. I was terrified and I do not get like this.

'The Queen is doing presentations today,' our escort announced.

That made it extra special.

It seemed as though I was waiting and waiting and then finally somebody called my name.

Wow. This was it. I walked off into a massive hall. I was standing at the back. I could see Her Majesty to my right. I spotted my wife too. But that is all I could make out. I stood behind a wall and then there was another queue. I only knew that I was getting nearer and nearer but it felt like one of those rides at a Disney park when you think it must be your turn around the next corner and it still isn't. I didn't really absorb what was being said ahead of me except being able to isolate the soundtrack that was the calling of my name.

Then it came. There was no preparation for this moment. I was aware the Queen might say something. Rumour suggested that she always had a few chosen words for every individual and on her nod, I stepped back.

'It must have been really satisfying saving those children,' she committed.

'It gave me a lot of pleasure, 'I replied without really knowing what I was saying and probably still dazzled by her knowledge of the detail that she offered freely and without script.

It was an extraordinarily polished performance. I played only a supporting role.

And it was done.

I turned to the right and headed off out of sight. Almost instantly, somebody took my award from me and put it in a box. You weren't really in a position to argue and off I walked outside slowly towards a band playing in front of the Gurkhas. You just followed the crowd, drifting without really knowing where to go.

My head was spinning, ecstatic that she knew why I was there – of course she did. I was relieved too that I was only listed as Ian James, Detective Sergeant so for the majority my anonymity was preserved but in the context of the day everybody was asking each other what each had received their award for and I felt comfortable enough or relieved of tension to finally utter those words:

'For saving children from child abuse'.

And one individual simply replied:

'This is for all the children you saved.'

Only then did I have a tear in my eye. It had taken that and all this time to finally extract any genuine emotion that affected me outside of the care for the individual child in the job.

By September a scroll arrived with Elizabeth R on it. There was an opportunity to get a DVD of the day too showing everything from your arrival to taking your seat and the camera on you as you meet The Queen.

I would imagine the uptake on this was universal because I could barely remember the day. It left me shattered more so than in any of the roles I had undertaken that had got me here. Something that had pre-occupied me for almost a week before we went to London left me with very few memories beyond exhaustion.

I am sure everybody would say the same. And no matter how many times I might watch that recording back, for a man whose primary undercover technique was his skill in recall and communication, I remained speechless and with almost no memory of the day.

All I could hear were the words the Queen spoke to me and in the years that followed they never left me:

'It must have been really satisfying saving all those children.'

And it was. It really was.

Then I remembered too:

'This is for all the children you saved.'

Julie had been with me throughout. Without her strength and dedication, it would have been impossible. I owe much too to my now late friend and mentor George. He had been right.

It was all about the children.

Save one child.

The End

ACKNOWLEDGEMENTS

Firstly, I would like to thank my good friend 'George' who mentored me through the early stages, and to whom I owe this story. Your words and wisdom remained with me. George sadly passed away a few years ago.

Equally to my other colleagues, there were so few of us with this unique specialism, but my respect is immense for the work you undertook.

To my wife, Julie, to whom I owe so much, always there supporting and understanding the sensitivity of my work, constantly keeping me grounded during difficult times, and maintaining a line that home is home with our children Emma and Michael.

To those senior investigating officers making ethical, moral and brave decisions without losing sight of the safety of the child.

I would also like to express my gratitude to the actor, Phillip Middlemass, who encouraged me to write my story and introduced me to my Editor, Tony Horne, who night after night strived to uncover every detail, yet knew the importance of preserving those captured within it.

Of course, there would be no book without a publisher, and to Rod Glenn and his team at Wild Wolf Publishing, thank you.

The last word goes to those victims and parents; I have done everything to protect your identities within this book. Your bravery, integrity and recovery, like the many others out there, I hope you and the supporting organisations have enabled you to move forward with your lives.

I dedicate this book to you.

Ian James MBE
November 2018

ABOUT THE AUTHOR

Ian James was born in October 1959 near Penzance in Cornwall. By 1977, he had moved to London, quickly rising through the ranks to the role of Detective and running informants.

By the late 1980s his personal life took him North to Cleveland when he continued in the role of a detective running informants on the Regional Crime Squad and National Crime Squad to infiltrate the underworld. Drugs and gun were on his watch.

Then, a chance meeting with an old friend changed his life forever. Would he like to be part of a team of just four, setting up a brand-new unit working in a dark and challenging world?

That meant for the next two decades he would assume a new identity. For the purpose of the role, Ian became a paedophile. The result is that he saved dozens of children from abuse and sent back to prison many who were a danger to society.

After retiring from the police in 2011, he now lives in North Yorkshire and is a Crime Trainer in criminal Investigation Modules.

For his services to the police, he was awarded an M.B.E.

SAVE ONE CHILD

SAVE ONE CHILD

CPSIA information can be obtained
at www.ICGtesting.com
Printed in the USA
BVHW070004201118
533516BV00001B/66/P